McGraw-Hill's

500 SAT
Math Questions

to know by test day

Also in McGraw-Hill's 500 Questions Series:

McGraw-Hill's

500 SAT
Math Questions

to know by test day

Jerimi Ann Walker

New York   Chicago   San Francisco   Athens   London   Madrid
Mexico City   Milan   New Delhi   Singapore   Sydney   Toronto

Jerimi Ann Walker is an assistant professor of mathematics at Moraine Valley Community College and a regular contributor to mathbootcamps.com.

1 2 3 4 5 6 7 8 9 10 11 12 13 14 15   QFR/QFR   1 0 9 8 7 6 5 4 3

ISBN   978-0-07-182061-5
MHID   0-07-182061-2

e-ISBN   978-0-07-182062-2
e-MHID   0-07-182062-0

Library of Congress Control Number 2013936204

SAT is a registered trademark of the College Entrance Examination Board, which was not involved in the production of, and does not endorse, this product.

Artwork by Cenveo

McGraw-Hill Education products are available at special quantity discounts to use as premiums and sales promotions or for use in corporate training programs. To contact a representative, please visit the "Contact Us" pages at www.mhprofessional.com.

This book is printed on acid-free paper.

CONTENTS

CONTENTS

INTRODUCTION

Congratulations! You've taken a big step toward SAT success by purchasing *McGraw-Hill's 500 SAT Math Questions to Know by Test Day*. We are here to help you take the next step and score high on your SAT exam so you can get into the college or university of your choice!

This book gives you 500 SAT-style questions that cover all the most essential math material. Each question is clearly explained in the answer key. The questions will give you valuable independent practice to supplement your regular textbook and the ground you have already covered in your math classes.

This book and the others in the series were written by expert teachers who know the SAT inside and out and can identify crucial information as well as the kinds of questions that are most likely to appear on the exam.

You might be the kind of student who needs to study extra a few weeks before the exam for a final review. Or you might be the kind of student who puts off preparing until the last minute before the exam. No matter what your preparation style, you will benefit from reviewing these 500 questions, which closely parallel the content, format, and degree of difficulty of the math questions on the actual SAT exam. These questions and the explanations in the answer key are the ideal last-minute study tool for those final weeks before the test.

If you practice with all the questions and answers in this book, we are certain you will build the skills and confidence needed to excel on the SAT. Good luck!

—*The Editors of McGraw-Hill Education*

CHAPTER 1

Numbers

1. When 21 is divided by j, the remainder is 3. If j is less than 9, what is the remainder when 30 is divided by j?

    (A) 12
    (B) 6
    (C) 5
    (D) 2
    (E) 0

2. The first term of a sequence is 2, and the remaining terms of the sequence are defined by the formula $a_n = 1 - a_{n-1}$ where a_n is the nth term of the sequence. What is the third term of the sequence?

    (A) −3
    (B) −2
    (C) −1
    (D) 2
    (E) 0

3. Suppose $3 \cdot 2^k = m$ where m is a positive integer larger than 45. What is the smallest possible value of m?

    (A) 46
    (B) 48
    (C) 120
    (D) 125
    (E) 216

4. The following pictogram shows the annual expenditure on park mainte-
   nance for a small town for three selected years. How much more was spent
   in 2000 than in 2010?

Annual Expenditure

2000	$ $ $ $
2005	$ $ $ $ $ $
2010	$ $ $

$ = 25,000 Dollars

   (A) $3,000
   (B) $5,000
   (C) $27,000
   (D) $50,000
   (E) $75,000

5. Let x represent 3.174 rounded to the nearest tenth and y represent 3.174
   rounded to the nearest hundredth. What is the value of $x + y$?

6. Suppose $m = 3 \cdot 8^{-2}$ and $n = 5 \cdot 8^{-2}$. What is the value of $m - n$?

   (A) $-\dfrac{1}{2084}$

   (B) $-\dfrac{1}{32}$

   (C) $-\dfrac{1}{16}$

   (D) $-\dfrac{1}{8}$

   (E) $-\dfrac{1}{4}$

7. What is the difference between the largest prime number less than 100 and
   the largest prime number less than 45?

8. Which of the following expressions is equivalent to $\sqrt[3]{27x^5}$?

(A) $9\sqrt[3]{3x^2}$

(B) $9x\sqrt[3]{x^2}$

(C) $9x\sqrt[3]{3x^2}$

(D) $3x\sqrt[3]{x^2}$

(E) $3\sqrt[3]{x^2}$

9. If $x = -1$, which of the following is the least in value?

(A) x^{-1}

(B) $-x^{-1}$

(C) x^{-2}

(D) $-2x^{-2}$

(E) $2x^{-2}$

10. If $8^{j/k} = 16$ and j and k are integers, what is the product of j and k?

(A) 2

(B) 3

(C) 6

(D) 12

(E) 18

11. On the number line shown, tick marks are equally spaced between zero and one. What is the value of $Q - P$?

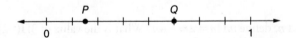

12. The first term of a sequence is 4, and each subsequent term is determined by multiplying the previous term by the integer m. If the third term of the sequence is 16 and the sixth term of the sequence is -128, what is the value of m?

13. Define $a \nabla b$ as $\dfrac{a-b}{b}$ for any integers a, b. If the value of $a \nabla 4$ is a positive integer less than 40, what is the largest possible value of a?

14. There are 19 students enrolled in a history class and 24 students enrolled in a physics class. If 7 students are enrolled in both courses, how many are enrolled in only one of the courses?

    (A) 43
    (B) 36
    (C) 29
    (D) 28
    (E) 19

15. The chart shown indicates the total sales in thousands of dollars for two different locations of a pizza restaurant. According to the chart, which of the following is the closest to the total sales in July and August at the Jefferson City location?

    (A) $72,000
    (B) $76,000
    (C) $79,000
    (D) $85,000
    (E) $89,000

16. For integers m and n, define $m \Pi n = 2m - 4n$. What is the value of $3\Pi(-2)$?

    (A) −16
    (B) −2
    (C) 3
    (D) 4
    (E) 14

17. Suppose x is a positive integer. What is the smallest value of x that makes the following inequality true?

$$|1 - 2x| < 3$$

18. The values of $\sqrt{4a}$ and $2b^{\frac{1}{2}}$ are the same. If a represents the smallest prime number, what is the value of b?

    (A) 2

    (B) 3

    (C) 8

    (D) 9

    (E) 12

19. Suppose the remainder when x is divided by 3, 4, or 11 is zero. Which of the following numbers must x be a multiple of?

    (A) 6

    (B) 8

    (C) 15

    (D) 16

    (E) 47

20. If $n^4 = 144$, what is the value of n^2?

    (A) 12

    (B) 36

    (C) 72

    (D) 122

    (E) 288

21. On the number line shown, the tick marks are evenly spaced between zero and one. What is the value of a?

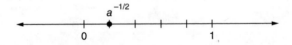

    (A) $\dfrac{1}{5}$

    (B) $\dfrac{1}{4}$

    (C) 10

    (D) 16

    (E) 25

22. A firm suggests that its employees spend between 8 and 14 hours a week on each of their assigned cases. If h represents the number of hours, which of the following inequalities would best represent this suggestion?

    (A) $|h-3|<11$

    (B) $|h-6|<14$

    (C) $|h-6|<8$

    (D) $|h-11|<3$

    (E) $|h-14|<8$

23. Suppose a, b, and c are positive real numbers. Which of the following expressions is/are equivalent to $14a = b^2c^6$?

    I. $a = \dfrac{(bc^3)^2}{14}$

    II. $14a = (bc^4)^2$

    III. $ab^{-2} = \dfrac{c^6}{14}$

    (A) I only

    (B) II only

    (C) III only

    (D) I and II only

    (E) I and III only

24. Suppose m, n, and p represent numbers such that $-1 < m < 0 < n < 1 < p$. Which of the following has the smallest value?

    (A) mn

    (B) mp

    (C) np

    (D) m^2

    (E) n^2

25. Let $x(\therefore)y$ be defined as $3xy$ and ∂x as $5z - 1$ for integers x and y. Suppose $5x(\therefore)2 = 2y$ and $\partial x = 14$. What is the value of $3y$?

    (A) 270

    (B) 135

    (C) 48

    (D) 45

    (E) 30

26. If $|4x - 9| = 19$ and x is a positive integer, what is the value of x?

    (A) 2
    (B) 6
    (C) 7
    (D) 8
    (E) 10

27. If $m = \left(\dfrac{p}{q}\right)^4$ and $n = \left(\dfrac{q}{p}\right)^{-2}$, what is the value of $\dfrac{m}{n}$?

    (A) −1
    (B) 1
    (C) $\left(\dfrac{p}{q}\right)^2$
    (D) $\left(\dfrac{p}{q}\right)^6$
    (E) $\left(\dfrac{p}{q}\right)^8$

28. Let x represent a real number that is a multiple of 6 and divisible by 14. If $x < 100$, what is the largest possible value of x?

29. Let A represent the set of positive multiples of 2 that are less than 10, and let B represent the set of positive multiples of 5 that are less than 20. How many numbers are in both sets?

    (A) 0
    (B) 1
    (C) 2
    (D) 3
    (E) 4

30. How much greater than $3x - 16$ is $3x + 1$?

    (A) 1
    (B) 5
    (C) 15
    (D) 17
    (E) 20

31. The figure shown indicates the total number of customer service calls completed (in hundreds) by a group of customer service agents at the same company as measured over a four-week period. According to the chart, between which two consecutive weeks was there the greatest increase in the number of customer service calls completed?

Customer Service Calls Completed

```
     │
     │
     │           ┌─┐
20 ─ │           │ │
     │           │ │  ┌─┐
15 ─ │           │ │  │ │  ┌─┐
     │      ┌─┐  │ │  │ │  │ │
10 ─ │      │ │  │ │  │ │  │ │
     │  ┌─┐ │ │  │ │  │ │  │ │
 5 ─ │  │ │ │ │  │ │  │ │  │ │
     │  │ │ │ │  │ │  │ │  │ │
     └──┴─┴─┴─┴──┴─┴──┴─┴──┴─┴──
       Week Week Week Week Week
        1    2    3    4    5
```

(A) Week 1 and Week 2
(B) Week 2 and Week 3
(C) Week 3 and Week 4
(D) Week 4 and Week 5
(E) This cannot be determined from the information given.

32. Let A represent the set of odd numbers greater than zero and smaller than 20 and B represent the set of whole numbers greater than 15 and smaller than 30. How many prime numbers are in the intersection of A and B?

(A) 0
(B) 1
(C) 2
(D) 5
(E) 10

33. On the number line shown, the tick marks are equally spaced. What is the value of K?

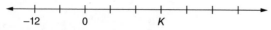

34. If $\sqrt{n} > 5$ for a positive integer n, then for an integer $m > 1$, $\sqrt[m]{n}$ must be larger than which of the following?

(A) 5

(B) $5\sqrt{n}$

(C) $\sqrt[m]{5}$

(D) $\sqrt[m]{5n}$

(E) This cannot be determined from the information given.

35. The nth term of a sequence a_n is defined by the formula $a_n = \dfrac{a_{n-1}}{2}$. If the fifth term of the sequence is 10, what is the first term of the sequence?

(A) $\dfrac{1}{32}$

(B) $\dfrac{1}{10}$

(C) 5

(D) 20

(E) 160

36. If $|x - 5| < 7$, which of the following is a possible value of x?

(A) −12

(B) −10

(C) 0

(D) 15

(E) 35

37. The integer j is a multiple of 7 and of $4k$, where k is a positive integer. Which of following is a possible value of j?

(A) −56

(B) −11

(C) 14

(D) 16

(E) 35

38. In the following sets, how many numbers are in set A but not in set B?
$A = \{1, 3, 5, 14, 21\}$
$B = \{0, 1, 4, 5, 16, 19\}$

    (A) Two
    (B) Three
    (C) Four
    (D) Five
    (E) Six

39. Let a represent 2.144 rounded to the nearest tenth. What is the value of $5a$?

40. Which of the following is equivalent to $a^n \cdot a^{-n} \cdot b^{2n}$ for positive integers a, b, and n?
    (A) 0
    (B) 1
    (C) ab
    (D) b^{2n}
    (E) $(ab)^{2n}$

41. If $(xy)^2 = 36$, each of the following is a possible value of $x + y$ EXCEPT
    (A) −6
    (B) −1
    (C) 5
    (D) 7
    (E) $\dfrac{25}{2}$

42. What is the value of $|-7 - 1|$?
    (A) −8
    (B) −7
    (C) 6
    (D) 7
    (E) 8

43. Suppose m is an odd integer greater than 10. What is the remainder when m is divided by 2?

44. The nth term of a sequence a_n is determined by the formula $a_n = \frac{1}{k}a_{n-1}$. If $a_1 = 100$, $a_3 = 1$, and k is a positive number, what is the value of k?

45. Suppose a is a positive integer such that $b = \frac{|-3a|}{a}$. Which of the following is a possible value of b?

(A) -3

(B) -1

(C) $-\dfrac{1}{2}$

(D) 0

(E) $\dfrac{1}{5}$

46. Suppose $j = \dfrac{1}{4^{-2}}$ and $k = \dfrac{3}{2^{-1}}$. What is the value of jk?

(A) $-\dfrac{3}{16}$

(B) $\dfrac{3}{32}$

(C) $\dfrac{3}{2}$

(D) 96

(E) 129

47. Let $a[\![\ ]\!]b = \dfrac{2a}{b}$ for real numbers a and b. Which of the following is the value of a if $a[\![\ ]\!](-4) = 3$?

(A) -12

(B) -8

(C) -6

(D) -1

(E) 4

48. If m is a prime number greater than 10, then how many distinct prime factors must $21m$ have?

(A) One

(B) Two

(C) Three

(D) Four

(E) Five

49. If $a < 0$, then which of the following must also be less than zero?

    I. $\dfrac{-1}{a^3}$

    II. $a + 10$

    III. $2a^{-1}$

(A) I only

(B) II only

(C) III only

(D) I and II only

(E) I, II, and III

50. Which of the following expressions is equivalent to $\left(\dfrac{2}{3} m^3 n^{\frac{1}{2}} \right)^2$ for all integer values of m and n?

(A) $\dfrac{4}{9} m^6 n$

(B) $\dfrac{2}{3} m^6 n$

(C) $\dfrac{4}{9} m^5 n^{\frac{5}{2}}$

(D) $\dfrac{4}{3} m^5 n^{\frac{5}{2}}$

(E) $\dfrac{2}{3} m^5 n^{\frac{5}{2}}$

51. On the number line shown, the tick marks are equally spaced. What is the value of A?

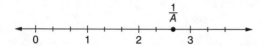

52. Suppose $4^{3a} = 16^{2b}$. If $a = 1$, what is the value of b?

53. Let A represent the set of positive multiples of 5, and let B represent the set of positive multiples of 35. How many numbers are in set A but NOT in set B?

   (A) 0

   (B) 2

   (C) 6

   (D) 30

   (E) Infinitely many

54. The following picture represents the total monthly attendance to a live music venue's concerts for three selected months. How many more people attended the venue's concerts in May than in January?

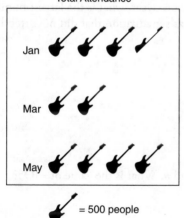

   (A) 250

   (B) 500

   (C) 1,750

   (D) 2,000

   (E) 3,750

55. Define $x\langle\ \rangle y$ as $\dfrac{1}{2}x^2 - y^2$ for real numbers x and y. What is the value of $(-4)\langle\ \rangle(-1)$?

(A) -5

(B) -3

(C) -1

(D) 7

(E) 9

56. Let a, b, c represent real numbers such that $a < 0 < b < c$. Which of the following inequalities must also be true?

   I. $a^2 < b^2 < c^2$
  II. $c - b > a$
 III. $c + a > b$

(A) I only

(B) II only

(C) III only

(D) I and II only

(E) I and III only

57. Last year, 54 of a school's 60 teachers attended graduation. If the school has replaced 2 retired teachers in the past year, what is the largest number of teachers who could attend this year's graduation that did not attend last year's?

(A) 2

(B) 4

(C) 6

(D) 8

(E) 14

58. Let $a\Theta b = \dfrac{-(a+b)}{a}$ for integers a and b. What is the value of $-1\Theta5$?

59. If $\left|-(-x)^2\right| = 9$, what is a possible value of x?

    (A) -3

    (B) $-\dfrac{1}{9}$

    (C) $\dfrac{5}{2}$

    (D) 6

    (E) 9

60. If $a = \dfrac{y}{x}$ and $b = \dfrac{x^2}{y^2}$ where x and y are nonzero, which of the following is equivalent to ab?

    (A) $\dfrac{x}{y}$

    (B) $\dfrac{y}{x}$

    (C) $\dfrac{x^3}{y}$

    (D) $\dfrac{x}{y^3}$

    (E) $\dfrac{y^3}{x^3}$

61. If n is a multiple of 11, which of the following must also be multiples of 11?

    I. $10n$

    II. n^2

    III. $\dfrac{n}{11}$

    (A) I only

    (B) II only

    (C) III only

    (D) I and II only

    (E) I, II, and III

62. Suppose a number m has four distinct prime factors, each larger than 7. How many prime factors will the number $6m$ have?

    (A) Four
    (B) Five
    (C) Six
    (D) Seven
    (E) This cannot be determined from the information given.

63. If the equation $2|a - b| = |b - a|$ is true, which of the following must be true?

    (A) The values of a and b sum to 1.
    (B) The values of a and b are the same.
    (C) The value of b is larger than the value of a.
    (D) The value of a is larger than the value of b.
    (E) The equation will hold for all real values of a and b.

64. Suppose for real numbers m and n, $m^2 < m$ and $n > 0$. Which of the following inequalities must be true?

    (A) $mn < 0$
    (B) $\dfrac{n}{m} > n$
    (C) $mn > n$
    (D) $n^2 < n$
    (E) $n^2 > m^2$

65. What is the largest prime factor of 270?

66. If the sum of two consecutive odd integers is divided by 2, what is the value of the remainder?

    (A) 0
    (B) 1
    (C) 2
    (D) 3
    (E) 4

67. The bar graph shown represents the percentage of movies owned by a particular family. Which of the following pie charts best represents the information provided?

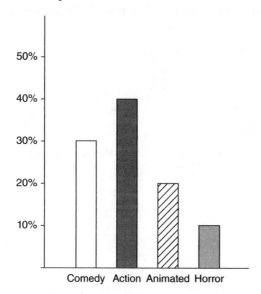

Comedy Action Animated Horror

(A)
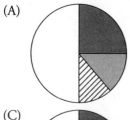

(B)
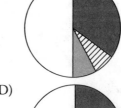

(C)
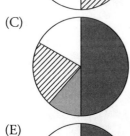

(D)

(E)
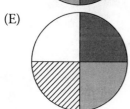

68. If x is a positive integer such that $\left(\dfrac{x}{3}\right)^2 = 9$, what is the value of x^{-1}?

69. If $\dfrac{n-1}{5}$ is a positive integer, what is the smallest possible integer value of n?

(A) 4
(B) 5
(C) 6
(D) 7
(E) 8

70. If x has prime factors 3, 5, and 19, then x must be divisible by each of the following EXCEPT

(A) 3
(B) 8
(C) 15
(D) 57
(E) 95

71. If for nonzero values of a and b, $(a)\Phi(b) = \left(\dfrac{2a}{b^2}\right)^{-3}$, then which of the following is equivalent to $(a^2)\Phi(4a)$?

(A) $\dfrac{1}{2a^3}$

(B) $\dfrac{a^3}{2}$

(C) $8a^3$

(D) 64

(E) 512

CHAPTER 2

Algebra

72. If $x - 2 = 14$, what is the value of x?

    (A) 2

    (B) 7

    (C) 12

    (D) 16

    (E) 28

73. The sum of two consecutive integers is 75. What is the value of the smaller integer?

    (A) 24

    (B) 29

    (C) 37

    (D) 41

    (E) 74

74. If $4ab = 24$, what is the value of $(2ab)^2$?

    (A) 16

    (B) 24

    (C) 48

    (D) 144

    (E) 576

75. Which of the following expressions best represents this statement? "The difference of two numbers is 7 less than the sum of the same two numbers."

    (A) $a - b = a + b - 7$
    (B) $a - b - 7 = a + b$
    (C) $a - b = ab - 7$
    (D) $a - b - 7 = ab$
    (E) $a - b - 7 = a + b + 7$

76. If for an integer a, $3x^2 = 2a$, then what is the value of $(3x - a)(3x + a)$ in terms of a?

    (A) $3a^2$
    (B) $4a$
    (C) $9a^2$
    (D) $2a + a^2$
    (E) $6a - a^2$

77. Bobby is 6 years older than Gina, and Gina is 4 years older than Ann. How many years older than Ann is Bobby?

    (A) 4
    (B) 6
    (C) 10
    (D) 12
    (E) 14

78. Let x and y be nonzero real numbers. If $2xy = 7(m + n)$ and $2(m + n) = 8$, what is the value of x in terms of y?

    (A) $\dfrac{14}{y}$

    (B) $\dfrac{28}{y}$

    (C) $\dfrac{8}{7y}$

    (D) $\dfrac{13}{2y}$

    (E) $\dfrac{11}{2y}$

79. Which of the following represents the solution set of $-3x + 2 < -2x + 4$?

(A) $x > -2$

(B) $x < -2$

(C) $-2 < x < -\dfrac{6}{5}$

(D) $x > -\dfrac{6}{5}$

(E) $x < -\dfrac{6}{5}$

80. The chess club decides to sell T-shirts to raise money for an upcoming tournament. On the first day, they sell 14 large T-shirts and 10 small T-shirts, raising a total of $248. On the second day, they sell only 6 large and 2 small T-shirts, raising an additional $88. How much did the club charge for the small T-shirts?

(A) $4

(B) $6

(C) $8

(D) $10

(E) $12

81. If $2x + 6y = 18$, what is the value of $x + 3y$?

(A) 5

(B) 6

(C) 7

(D) 8

(E) 9

82. If $x > 0$, $y > 0$, $x^2 = 9$, and $xy = 12$, then $(x - 2y)^2 =$

(A) -30

(B) -23

(C) 17

(D) 25

(E) 41

83. The value of an integer m is three times the value of an integer n, while the value of an integer k is twice the value of n. What is the value of k in terms of m?

   (A) $\dfrac{1}{6}m$

   (B) $\dfrac{3}{2}m$

   (C) $\dfrac{2}{3}m$

   (D) $5m$

   (E) $6m$

84. A student sets his budget for electricity at $\$x$. If for each of n days, he uses $\$k$ worth of electricity, which of the following expressions represents the amount left in his budget?

   (A) $x - n$

   (B) $x - k$

   (C) $nx - k$

   (D) $x - nk$

   (E) $n(x - k)$

85. A company rents graphing calculators for $15 a month for the first 3 months and then $10 for each of the following months. If a student rents a calculator for 9 months, how much will she pay in rental fees?

   (A) $45

   (B) $60

   (C) $90

   (D) $105

   (E) $135

86. The sum of two positive numbers is 28, while the difference of the same two numbers is 16. What is the value of the product of the two numbers?

87. If $xy = 32$ and $y = 4$, then $\dfrac{1}{4}x =$

   (A) 2

   (B) 3

   (C) 4

   (D) 5

   (E) 6

88. If $(a - b)(a + b) = 6$ and $a^2 = 8$, what is the value of b^2?

89. A number is 3 larger than the sum of 8 and 12. What is the value of the number?

90. Which of the following values of x satisfy the inequality $-5 < 2x < 7$?

(A) -3

(B) -2

(C) 4

(D) 7

(E) 14

91. If a, b, x, and y are positive numbers such that $a = 2x + 4y$ and $b = x + 2y$, how many times larger than b is a?

(A) $\dfrac{1}{4}$

(B) $\dfrac{1}{2}$

(C) 1

(D) 2

(E) 4

92. Let $x \oplus y = \dfrac{x + y^2}{x}$ for all nonzero values of x and all real values of y.

Which of the following is equivalent to $(2xy) \oplus (4xy)$?

(A) $4xy$

(B) $9x^2 y^2$

(C) $16x^2 y^2$

(D) $1 + 2xy$

(E) $1 + 8xy$

93. A cargo ship travels at a speed of m miles per hour when it is over the open ocean. Which of the following expressions represents the number of miles the cargo ship travels in n minutes?

    (A) $\dfrac{m}{60n}$

    (B) $\dfrac{nm}{60}$

    (C) $60nm$

    (D) $60n + m$

    (E) $60(n + m)$

94. If $\dfrac{\sqrt{x+1}}{4} = \dfrac{2}{3}$, then $x + 1 =$

    (A) $\dfrac{3}{64}$

    (B) $\dfrac{4}{9}$

    (C) $\dfrac{8}{3}$

    (D) $\dfrac{16}{3}$

    (E) $\dfrac{64}{9}$

95. If $xy^2 = 4$, what is the value of $\dfrac{2x^3 y^4 - x^2 y^2}{x^2 y^2}$?

    (A) 3

    (B) 4

    (C) 7

    (D) 8

    (E) 11

96. Which of the following is equivalent to $9m^2 - 6m + 1$?

    (A) $3m + 1$

    (B) $3m - 1$

    (C) $(3m + 1)^2$

    (D) $(3m - 1)^2$

    (E) $3m^2 + 1$

97. Suppose p, q, r, and s are nonzero real numbers. If $pq = r$ and $q = \dfrac{s}{p}$, which of the following is equivalent to r?

(A) 0

(B) 1

(C) s

(D) $p^2 s$

(E) $\dfrac{p}{s}$

98. A bag of coins contains three times as many pennies as nickels. When 10 nickels are added to the bag, there are 14 fewer nickels than pennies. In total, how many nickels and pennies are in the bag?

(A) 12

(B) 36

(C) 48

(D) 108

(E) 144

99. If $\dfrac{1}{4}\sqrt{x} = 8$, then $\dfrac{7}{4}\sqrt{x} = ?$

100. A store clerk earns $11.50 an hour before taxes. Next year, the clerk will be given a raise of $1.25 each hour. If he works h hours a week, which of the following represents his weekly wage after the raise?

(A) $12.75h$

(B) $11.5h + 1.25$

(C) $11.5 + 1.25h$

(D) $\dfrac{12.75}{h}$

(E) $\dfrac{11.5}{1.25h}$

101. If $\dfrac{2}{3}a \geq 1$, which of the following is a possible value of a?

(A) $\dfrac{1}{9}$

(B) $\dfrac{1}{3}$

(C) 0

(D) 1

(E) 2

102. If $2x^2 - y + 1 = 15$, what is the value of $2x^2 - y - 7$?

(A) −7

(B) −6

(C) 7

(D) 8

(E) 21

103. The value of an integer is $\frac{1}{8}$ th the value of another integer. If both integers are larger than 1, what is the smallest possible value of the smaller integer?

104. Gary gave away half of his baseball card collection and was left with 120 fewer baseball cards than he originally had. How many baseball cards were in his collection before he gave any away?

(A) 60

(B) 120

(C) 240

(D) 480

(E) 960

105. Which of the following is 8 more than $\dfrac{x+1}{y}$ for nonzero values of x and y?

(A) $\dfrac{x+9}{y}$

(B) $\dfrac{9x+1}{y}$

(C) $\dfrac{x+1}{y+8}$

(D) $\dfrac{x+8y+1}{y}$

(E) $\dfrac{x+8y+1}{8y}$

106. If a is any positive integer, how many solutions to $-2 < x + 5 < 9$ can be written in the form $3a$?

(A) Zero

(B) One

(C) Two

(D) Three

(E) Four

107. If $2x - 7 = x + 1$, what is the value of x?

(A) −6

(B) 1

(C) 4

(D) 7

(E) 8

108. A certain spice mixture stays fresh for 3 months. A restaurant purchased 3 pounds of the mixture last month and 2 pounds this month. If the spice mixture is stored and not used, how many pounds will still be fresh in 4 months?

(A) 0

(B) 1

(C) 2

(D) 3

(E) 5

109. Which of the following represents the product of two consecutive odd integers m and n when $m < n$?

(A) $m^2 + 1$

(B) $m^2 + m$

(C) $m^2 + 2m$

(D) $m^2 + 2m + 1$

(E) $m^2 + 2m - 1$

110. If a is 10 more than b and b is 7 less than c, which of the following represents the value of a in terms of c?

(A) $c - 7$

(B) $c - 3$

(C) $c + 3$

(D) $c + 7$

(E) $c + 17$

111. If $x - 4y = 15$ and $2x + 6y = 16$, what is the value of x?

112. The square of a nonzero number is equal to one-half the number. What is the value of the number?

113. Which of the following is equivalent to $\left(\dfrac{1}{5}x - y\right)^2$?

(A) $\dfrac{1}{5}(x^2 - y^2)$

(B) $\dfrac{1}{25}x^2 - y^2$

(C) $\dfrac{1}{25}x^2 + y^2$

(D) $\dfrac{1}{25}x^2 - \dfrac{2}{5}xy + y^2$

(E) $\dfrac{1}{25}x^2 + \dfrac{1}{10}xy + y^2$

114. A large recipe requires $20\dfrac{1}{2}$ pounds of flour. If flour can only be purchased in 50-pound bags, how many bags of flour must be purchased in order to make the recipe 8 times?

(A) 2

(B) 3

(C) 4

(D) 5

(E) 8

115. Given that the square root of the sum of m and n is equal to the product of 4 and m, which of the following is equivalent to $m + n$?

(A) $4m$

(B) $16m^2$

(C) $4m - n^2$

(D) $4(m - n)^2$

(E) $16(m^2 - n^2)$

116. The value of $\dfrac{a}{b}$ is 6. What is the value of $\dfrac{2a}{3b}$?

(A) 2

(B) 4

(C) 8

(D) 12

(E) 18

117. A company designs a box that can store c specialty game pieces for its latest board game. If 5 such game pieces are stored in the box, which of the following represents the number of pieces that can still be stored in the box?

(A) $c - 5$

(B) $c + 5$

(C) $5c$

(D) $\dfrac{c}{5}$

(E) $\dfrac{c - 5}{c}$

118. If $2xy = 26$ and $0 < x < 4$, which of the following is NOT a possible value of y?

(A) 3

(B) 5

(C) 8

(D) 12

(E) 14

119. If $-9x \le -28$, what is the smallest possible integer value of x?

120. If $\dfrac{1}{4} = \dfrac{3}{a} + \dfrac{1}{7}$, what is the value of a?

121. Which of the following must be larger than $a^2 - 2ab$ for all real values of a and b?

I. $(a-b)^2$

II. $a(a-2b)$

III. $a-2b$

(A) I only

(B) II only

(C) III only

(D) I and III only

(E) I, II, and III

122. A number m is two times as large as a number n. If n is 5 more than 8, what is the value of m?

123. A set of numbers contains 40 multiples of 2, of which $\dfrac{1}{4}$ are also multiples of 3. If the set contains half as many multiples of 5 as it contains multiples of 3, how many total numbers are in the set?

(A) 45

(B) 55

(C) 80

(D) 195

(E) 280

124. If $\dfrac{1}{2}x = \dfrac{1}{4}y$, what is $\dfrac{3}{4}x + 1$ in terms of y?

(A) $3y+1$

(B) $\dfrac{1}{2}y+1$

(C) $\dfrac{3}{8}y+1$

(D) $\dfrac{1}{2}y+\dfrac{1}{2}$

(E) $\dfrac{3}{8}y+\dfrac{3}{8}$

125. Let $m \ominus n = 3m^2 - n$. If $2 \ominus n = 9$, what is the value of n?

    (A) −12

    (B) −11

    (C) −3

    (D) 3

    (E) 12

126. If $x - 2y = 8$, what is the value of $\dfrac{x}{2} - y$?

    (A) 2

    (B) 4

    (C) 10

    (D) 12

    (E) 16

127. For all values of a, how much larger is $6a + 5$ than $6a - 3$?

    (A) 2

    (B) 3

    (C) 5

    (D) 7

    (E) 8

128. If x is a solution to $3 < 2m + 1 < 10$, then which of the following CANNOT be a solution to the inequality?

    I. $\dfrac{1}{2}x$

    II. $2x$

    III. $5x$

    (A) I only

    (B) II only

    (C) III only

    (D) I and II only

    (E) I and III only

129. An urn contains 6 more green marbles than it contains red marbles. If the number of red marbles is represented by r, which of the following expressions represents the total number of marbles in the urn?

(A) $6r$

(B) $r+6$

(C) $2r+6$

(D) $2r+12$

(E) r^2+6

130. If $x-2=4x-6$, what is the value of x?

131. If $4p+q=k$ and $p=2q$, then in terms of p and q, k also equals

(A) $3q$

(B) $9q$

(C) $9pq$

(D) $8p+q$

(E) $8p+2q$

132. Which of the following is half as large as $\dfrac{3x}{y}+\dfrac{1}{6}$ for all nonzero values of x and y?

(A) $\dfrac{x+2y}{6y}$

(B) $\dfrac{6x+y}{4y}$

(C) $\dfrac{3x+y}{12y}$

(D) $\dfrac{18x+y}{6y}$

(E) $\dfrac{18x+y}{12y}$

133. A student can run 5 miles in 36 minutes. If the student maintains the same speed, how many miles can he run in 45 minutes?

(A) $\dfrac{1}{9}$

(B) $\dfrac{5}{36}$

(C) $\dfrac{5}{4}$

(D) $\dfrac{10}{4}$

(E) $\dfrac{25}{4}$

134. If $2ab - a = 5$, then what is the value of $4ab - 2a + 4$?

135. How many positive integers are in the solution set of $3x < \dfrac{11}{2}$ and $-2 < x + 1 < 4$?

(A) None

(B) One

(C) Two

(D) Three

(E) Four

136. For what nonzero values of m and n is the inequality $(m + n)^2 \leq (m - n)^2$ true?

(A) When $m > 0$ and $n > 0$

(B) When $m < 0$ and $n < 0$

(C) When m and n have opposite signs

(D) When m is twice as large as n

(E) This cannot be determined from the information given.

137. If $\sqrt{x - 1} = \dfrac{1}{4}$, then what does $x =$?

138. If $a = 4b$ and $a > 14$, then which of the following must be true?

(A) $b > \dfrac{7}{2}$

(B) $b > \dfrac{5}{2}$

(C) $b > 4$

(D) $b > 10$

(E) $b > 56$

139. If $3m - n = 10$ and $-2m + 4n = 8$, what is the value of $m + 3n$?

(A) 2

(B) $\dfrac{24}{5}$

(C) $\dfrac{39}{5}$

(D) 10

(E) 18

140. Given that two-thirds of x is equivalent to the product of 5 and y, which of the following is equivalent to $15y$?

(A) $\dfrac{2}{9}x$

(B) $\dfrac{1}{3}x$

(C) $\dfrac{5}{3}x$

(D) $2x$

(E) $15x$

141. A single performance of a magic show requires the use of x envelopes, and the envelopes cannot be reused after a performance. Suppose the magician must perform her magic show y times this week. Which of the following expressions represents the number of envelopes she will need this week?

(A) $\dfrac{x}{y}$

(B) $\dfrac{y}{x}$

(C) xy

(D) $x + y$

(E) $x - y$

142. Which of the following is equivalent to $ab^3 - ab^4 + a^2b^2$?

(A) $ab(b^2 - b^3 + ab)$

(B) $ab(ab^2 - ab^3 + ab)$

(C) $ab(b^2 - b^3 + 1)$

(D) $ab(b^3 - b^4 + 1)$

(E) $ab(b^3 - b^4)$

CHAPTER 3

Probability, Statistics, and Sequences

143. What is the arithmetic mean of the numbers 5x, 3x, 2x, and 8x?

(A) $\dfrac{9x}{2}$

(B) 9x

(C) 12x

(D) 18x

(E) 36x

144. The probability of event A occurring is 0.25, and the probability of event B occurring is 0.30. If the two events are independent, what is the probability of both events occurring?

(A) 0.075

(B) 0.150

(C) 0.550

(D) 0.850

(E) This cannot be determined from the given information.

145. A set of integers contains all integers greater than 1 and less than 15. If an integer is randomly selected from this set, what is the probability it is smaller than 5?

(A) $\dfrac{1}{13}$

(B) $\dfrac{3}{13}$

(C) $\dfrac{5}{13}$

(D) $\dfrac{9}{13}$

(E) $\dfrac{10}{13}$

146. In a group of 80 people, the probability of selecting someone who is older than 25 is $\dfrac{3}{4}$. How many people in the group are 25 years old or younger?

147. What is the median of the following set of numbers? 12, 6, 1, 1, 4

(A) 1

(B) 3

(C) 4

(D) 5

(E) 6

148. A data set contains 8 numbers. If the mean of this data set is 4, what is the sum of the numbers in the data set?

(A) 4

(B) 8

(C) 16

(D) 32

(E) 64

149. A jar contains twice as many red coins as it does blue coins. If a coin is selected at random, what is the probability the coin is blue?

(A) $\dfrac{1}{6}$

(B) $\dfrac{1}{5}$

(C) $\dfrac{1}{4}$

(D) $\dfrac{1}{3}$

(E) $\dfrac{1}{2}$

150. How many passwords consisting of four digits between 0 and 9 inclusive are made up of all odd numbers?

(A) 4

(B) 16

(C) 24

(D) 256

(E) 625

151. The area of one circle is half the area of another circle. If the radius of the larger circle is r, which of the following expressions represents the average area of the two circles?

(A) $2\pi r^2$

(B) πr^2

(C) $\dfrac{\pi}{2}r^2$

(D) $\dfrac{3\pi}{4}r^2$

(E) $\dfrac{3\pi}{2}r^2$

152. The numbers n_1, n_2, n_3, n_4, n_5 are consecutive integers, and the median of the list is 3. What is the median of the list $n_1 + 5, n_2 + 5, n_3 + 5, n_4 + 5, n_5 + 5$?

(A) 6

(B) 7

(C) 8

(D) 9

(E) 10

153. Gregory has 15 different science fiction books and will randomly select 4 of these books to donate to charity. How many different possible ways can he select the 4 books?

(A) 19

(B) 60

(C) 974

(D) 1,365

(E) 32,760

154. The average of p, q, and r is 12. When the number m is included in the list, the average increases to 20. What is the value of m?

(A) 5

(B) 8

(C) 32

(D) 44

(E) 65

155. The 30th term of a geometric sequence is k, and each term of the sequence is found by multiplying the previous term by $\frac{1}{2}$. Which of the following represents the first term of the sequence in terms of k?

(A) $2^{29} \times k$

(B) $2^{30} \times k$

(C) $\dfrac{k}{2^{29}}$

(D) $\dfrac{k}{2^{30}}$

(E) $2^{30} + 2^{29} \times k$

156. The students in a classroom are either seniors or juniors, and exactly 15 of the students are seniors. If the probability of randomly selecting a senior from this classroom is $\frac{5}{9}$, how many students in the classroom are juniors?

(A) 5

(B) 12

(C) 15

(D) 27

(E) 34

157. The first three terms of a sequence are *a*, *b*, and *c*, respectively, and the next three terms of the sequence are also *a*, *b*, and *c*. If this pattern continues, which of the following would represent the sum of the 50th and the 90th terms?

(A) 2*a*

(B) 2*b*

(C) 2*c*

(D) *a* + *b*

(E) *b* + *c*

158. The numbers in the set {1, 4, 6, 8} are arranged into a four-digit number. If the number created is always less than 2,000, how many different arrangements are possible?

159. What is the average (arithmetic mean) of $2x$, $x + 4$, and 5?

(A) $x + 3$

(B) $x + 9$

(C) $3x + 3$

(D) $3x + 4$

(E) $3x + 9$

160. The median of a list of 10 integers is 14. When the integers are placed in order from smallest to largest, the fifth integer in the list is 11. What is the value of the sixth integer in the list?

161. The special at a restaurant consists of a choice of one appetizer, one entrée, and one dessert. There are twice as many choices for an appetizer as there are for entrées, and there are 5 more dessert choices than appetizer choices. If there are 4 choices for an appetizer, how many different possible specials can be ordered?

162. The average of a set of 10 numbers is *x*, while the average of a set of 10 different numbers is *y*. If the two sets are combined, which of the following represents the sum of the 20 numbers in terms of *x* and *y*?

(A) $x + y$

(B) $10x + y$

(C) $x + 10y$

(D) $10(x + y)$

(E) $x + y + 10$

163. In a line to claim a prize, Jackie is both 12th counting from the front of the line and 12th counting from the back of the line. How many people are in line to claim the prize?

(A) 12

(B) 20

(C) 22

(D) 23

(E) 24

164. The management at a theater sent out surveys to determine how many plays its previous patrons had attended in the last year. The results are shown in the following table. What is the median number of plays attended by patrons of this theater?

Survey of Theater Patrons

Number of Plays Attended	Number of Patrons
2	25
3	15
4	35
5	10
6	5
7	2

165. The average of three consecutive integers is 150. What is the median of these three integers?

166. If the median of 1, 4, 9, 12, and x is 9, then each of the following is a possible value of x EXCEPT

(A) 5

(B) 9

(C) 10

(D) 13

(E) 19

167. If 8 out of 64 coins in a purse are quarters, what is the probability a coin randomly selected from the purse will be a quarter?

(A) $\dfrac{1}{64}$

(B) $\dfrac{1}{9}$

(C) $\dfrac{1}{8}$

(D) $\dfrac{3}{4}$

(E) $\dfrac{8}{9}$

168. In a group of people, 150 of the people are younger than 38 years old, while 29 of the people are 38 years old or older. Which of the following must be true about the median age of people in this group?

(A) The median age is less than 38.

(B) The median age is 38.

(C) The median age is between 29 and 38.

(D) The median age is more than 38.

(E) The median age may be less or more than 38.

169. How many two-digit integers larger than 10 have a ones digit that is a multiple of 3?

(A) 12

(B) 27

(C) 64

(D) 81

(E) 240

170. In a certain game, points are awarded based on which integer is randomly selected from the integers 1, 2, 3, 4, 5, 6, 7, 8, 9, 10. If an even integer is selected, 5 points are awarded. Otherwise, 2 points are awarded. If the game is played once, what is the probability the player will earn 2 points?

171. The first term of a sequence is 104. The second term of the sequence is found by dividing the first term by 2, while the third term in a sequence is found by subtracting 4 from the second term. If these steps are repeated in this order, what is the first term that will have a value smaller than 1?

(A) 7th term

(B) 8th term

(C) 9th term

(D) 10th term

(E) 11th term

172. Joseph spends his time at school attending classes, attending football practice, and completing homework assignments. Typically, he will spend 7 hours in classes, 2 hours in football practice, and 1 hour completing homework. If a randomly selected time is chosen during a typical school day, what is the probability Joseph is NOT in classes?

(A) $\dfrac{1}{10}$

(B) $\dfrac{3}{10}$

(C) $\dfrac{2}{7}$

(D) $\dfrac{3}{7}$

(E) $\dfrac{5}{7}$

173. If the symbols α, β, and γ are randomly arranged in a row, what is the probability the symbol γ is first?

(A) $\dfrac{2}{27}$

(B) $\dfrac{1}{9}$

(C) $\dfrac{1}{6}$

(D) $\dfrac{1}{3}$

(E) $\dfrac{2}{3}$

174. Hilda is 3 years older than Frank, and Frank is 6 years younger than George. If George's age is represented by G, which of the following represents their average age in terms of G?

(A) G

(B) $3G$

(C) $G - 3$

(D) $G + 1$

(E) $3G - 9$

175. If 75% of the students in a class had an average test score of 82, while the remaining students in the class had an average test score of 79, what was the average test score for the entire class?

(A) 40.13

(B) 79.25

(C) 80.25

(D) 81.25

(E) 83.75

176. The median of 5 positive integers is 15. What is the smallest possible value of any of these integers?

177. Each term in a sequence of numbers is found by adding n to the previous term. If the first term of the sequence is x, which of the following represents the 19th term of the sequence?

(A) $19x + n$

(B) $x + 19n$

(C) $19(x + n)$

(D) $18x + n$

(E) $x + 18n$

178. In the following figure, each line segment represents a path of length 1 between the indicated points. How many different paths of length 2 are possible from A to C?

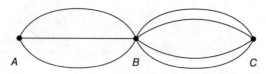

  (A) 4

  (B) 6

  (C) 9

  (D) 12

  (E) 16

179. Out of 9 members, a club must select 3 officers, each with a different rank. A club member may not be selected as an officer more than once. How many different ways can the three officers be selected?

  (A) 9

  (B) 27

  (C) 504

  (D) 729

  (E) 941

180. What is the probability a randomly generated two-digit number is less than 99?

181. What is the average (arithmetic mean) of $2x^2$ and $4x$?

  (A) $2x$

  (B) $3x^2$

  (C) $x^2 + 2x$

  (D) $x^2 + 4x$

  (E) $2x^2 + 4x + 2$

182. Two triangles share the same length base, but the height of one triangle is three times the height of the other. If the average area of the two triangles is 10, what is the area of the smaller triangle?

(A) $\dfrac{5}{2}$

(B) 5

(C) $\dfrac{20}{3}$

(D) 10

(E) 20

183. Each term of a sequence is found by multiplying a previous term by a fixed value r. If the fifth term of the sequence is 3,888 and the third term is 108, what is the value of r?

(A) 4

(B) 6

(C) 36

(D) 945

(E) 1,890

184. If the following steps are completed once, what is the probability the resulting remainder will be zero?

Step 1   Randomly select a number from the set {4, 6, 7, 14, 18, 21}.
Step 2   Subtract 2 from the selected number.
Step 3   Divide the number by 4 and determine the remainder.

(A) $\dfrac{1}{6}$

(B) $\dfrac{1}{3}$

(C) $\dfrac{1}{2}$

(D) $\dfrac{2}{3}$

(E) $\dfrac{5}{6}$

185. Half of the construction paper in a classroom is blue, while the other half is orange. A teacher brings in a new box of blue construction paper, bringing the total number of boxes of blue paper to 5. What is the probability a randomly selected box of paper is orange?

(A) $\dfrac{1}{5}$

(B) $\dfrac{1}{4}$

(C) $\dfrac{1}{2}$

(D) $\dfrac{4}{9}$

(E) $\dfrac{5}{9}$

186. An ice cream shop offers m types of ice cream, n types of syrup, and p types of toppings. How many different orders including one flavor of ice cream, one flavor of syrup, and one topping are possible?

(A) mnp

(B) $m + n + p$

(C) $m - n - p$

(D) $m(n-1)(p-2)$

(E) $m^3 n^2 p$

187. The first term of a sequence is 1. Each subsequent term of the sequence is found by multiplying the previous term by 5 and then subtracting 2. If a_n represents the nth term of the sequence, which of the following represents a formula for a_n where $n > 1$?

(A) $5a_{n-1} - 2$

(B) $5(a_{n-1} - 2)$

(C) $5a_n - 2$

(D) $5(a_n - 2)$

(E) $5a_{n-1} - 2a_n$

188. How many four-digit numbers smaller than 1,100 end in either a 5 or a 7?

189. A club with 20 members must select 2 who will act as ushers at an upcoming event. How many ways can the 2 ushers be selected?

(A) 190

(B) 260

(C) 380

(D) 400

(E) 420

190. If the median of $-2x$, x, and x^2 is $-2x$, which of the following can be a value of x?

(A) -4

(B) -2

(C) -1

(D) 1

(E) 2

191. In a single roll of a fair six-sided die, what is the probability a 3 comes up?

192. In how many ways can four of five different paintings be displayed in a row on a wall?

193. If $0 < x < 1$, what is the median of $3x$, x, x^3, x^2, and x^4?

(A) $3x$

(B) x

(C) x^3

(D) x^2

(E) x^4

194. The following figure represents a circle with center O that is divided into three segments: A, B, and C. If a point within the circle is randomly selected, what is the probability it will be in segment B?

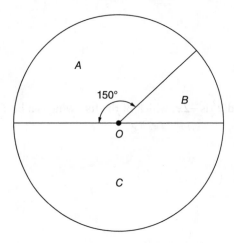

(A) $\dfrac{1}{12}$

(B) $\dfrac{1}{9}$

(C) $\dfrac{1}{6}$

(D) $\dfrac{1}{4}$

(E) $\dfrac{1}{3}$

195. The median time for 6 students to finish an exam was 1 hour and 25 minutes. In minutes, which of the following is the sum of the third and fourth fastest times?

(A) 42

(B) 70

(C) 85

(D) 170

(E) 255

196. A set contains 10 identical numbers. If that number is represented by n, which of the following statements must be true?

  I. The average of the 10 numbers is n.

  II. The median of the 10 numbers is n.

  III. The median of the 10 numbers is $\dfrac{n}{2}$.

  (A) I only
  (B) II only
  (C) III only
  (D) I and II
  (E) I and III

197. Two symbols from the set $\{\varepsilon, \varphi, \Delta, \Omega, \forall, \Pi\}$ are to be selected as part of generating a random password. Any symbol that is selected can be selected again. In how many ways can the two symbols be selected?

  (A) 2
  (B) 11
  (C) 12
  (D) 30
  (E) 36

198. The mean of a set of 15 unique numbers is 135. If the five largest numbers are removed from the set, which of the following statements must be true about the new set?

  (A) The mean will be 130.
  (B) The mean will remain 135.
  (C) The mean will be smaller than 135, but it may or may not be 130.
  (D) The mean will no longer be 135, but it may be smaller or larger than 135.
  (E) The mean will be larger than 135.

199. The mean of the data set $\{x_1, x_2, x_3, x_4, y_1, y_2, y_3\}$ is 6. If the mean of the set $\{x_1, x_2, x_3, x_4\}$ is 3, what is the mean of the set $\{y_1, y_2, y_3\}$?

  (A) 3
  (B) 4
  (C) 9
  (D) 10
  (E) 12

200. The probability of event A occurring is $\dfrac{x}{4}$, while the probability of event B occurring is $\dfrac{3x}{8}$. If the two events cannot occur at the same time, what is the probability event A or event B will occur?

(A) $\dfrac{x}{8}$

(B) $\dfrac{x}{3}$

(C) $\dfrac{5x}{8}$

(D) $\dfrac{3x^2}{32}$

(E) $\dfrac{3x^2}{8}$

201. If $y = 8$, what is the numerical value of the median of $3y, \dfrac{2}{3}y, 10y,$ and $\dfrac{7}{3}y$?

202. A data set consists of the number 1 n times and the number 3 one time. Which of the following statements must be true about the mean and the median?

(A) The mean and the median will equal 1.

(B) The mean will be larger than 1, and the median will be equal to 1.

(C) The mean will equal 1, and the median will be larger than 1.

(D) The mean and the median will be larger than 1.

(E) This cannot be determined from the information given.

203. Joe has kept track of how many new movies he has seen each year for the past five years. The greatest number of new movies he saw in these years was 20, while the median number of new movies he saw was 14. If the least number of new movies he saw in any of these years was 10, which of the following could be the average number of movies he has seen per year over the past five years?

(A) 8

(B) 10

(C) 12

(D) 13

(E) 15

204. The probability of selecting a random integer between the positive integers x and y inclusive is $\dfrac{1}{122}$. What is the smallest possible value of y?

205. If the pattern 1, 2, −1, 1, 2, −1, 4, 1, 2, −1, ... continues, what is the value of the 100th term in the sequence?

206. In a list of 8 numbers, each value is 10 more than the previous value. If the smallest value in the list is 15, what is the median of the list?

(A) 40

(B) 45

(C) 50

(D) 55

(E) 60

207. What is the probability a randomly generated three-digit integer will be less than 150 and have a ones digit of 7?

208. The average of $3x$, $5x$, $2x − 1$, and $x + 1$ is 8. What is the average of x and $x + 2$?

(A) $\dfrac{12}{11}$

(B) $\dfrac{32}{11}$

(C) $\dfrac{43}{11}$

(D) $\dfrac{48}{11}$

(E) $\dfrac{64}{11}$

209. The probability of randomly selecting a green marble from a jar containing green, red, and blue marbles is $\dfrac{2}{9}$. What is the probability of randomly selecting a red or blue marble from the jar?

(A) $\dfrac{1}{3}$

(B) $\dfrac{4}{9}$

(C) $\dfrac{2}{3}$

(D) $\dfrac{7}{9}$

(E) $\dfrac{11}{9}$

210. A school club has 3 freshmen, 2 sophomores, and 10 juniors as members. If a member is randomly selected to represent the club at an after-school function, what is the probability the selected member is a sophomore?

(A) $\dfrac{1}{15}$

(B) $\dfrac{2}{15}$

(C) $\dfrac{2}{13}$

(D) $\dfrac{1}{4}$

(E) $\dfrac{1}{2}$

211. What is the average of $\sqrt{2}$ and $5\sqrt{2}$?

(A) $\sqrt{2}$

(B) $3\sqrt{2}$

(C) 3

(D) $\dfrac{9}{2}$

(E) 6

212. The median of a list of 12 numbers is $\dfrac{7}{4}$. When the list of numbers is written in order from smallest to largest, the sixth and seventh numbers have the same value. What is the value of the sixth number?

213. The median of a set of six consecutive integers is $\dfrac{29}{2}$. What is the value of the smallest integer in the set?

Coordinate Geometry

214. What is the slope of a line that passes through the origin and the point $(-1, 5)$?

(A) -5

(B) $-\dfrac{1}{5}$

(C) 0

(D) $\dfrac{1}{5}$

(E) 5

215. Which of the following points is on the graph of the line $y = 3x - 1$?

(A) $(0, 0)$

(B) $(3, -1)$

(C) $(-3, 1)$

(D) $(1, 2)$

(E) $(4, 12)$

216. What is the equation of the line whose graph is perpendicular to the graph of the line $y = -\dfrac{2}{3}x + \dfrac{1}{5}$ and passes through the point $\left(0, \dfrac{1}{8}\right)$?

(A) $y = \dfrac{1}{8}x + \dfrac{1}{5}$

(B) $y = -\dfrac{2}{3}x + \dfrac{1}{8}$

(C) $y = -\dfrac{2}{3}x - 8$

(D) $y = \dfrac{3}{2}x + \dfrac{1}{8}$

(E) $y = \dfrac{3}{2}x - 8$

217. Which of the lines in the following figure has a slope closest to 0?

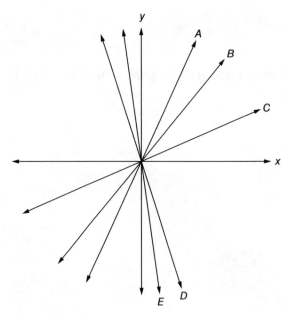

(A) Line *A*
(B) Line *B*
(C) Line *C*
(D) Line *D*
(E) Line *E*

218. In the following figure, $\overline{PQ}$ and $\overline{MN}$ have the same length. What is the value of x?

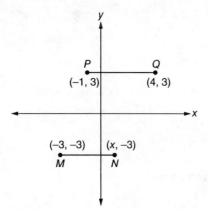

(A) −3

(B) −2

(C) 0

(D) 2

(E) 4

219. The line $y = mx$ passes through the point $(2, 8)$. What is the value of m?

(A) −6

(B) −4

(C) $-\dfrac{1}{4}$

(D) $\dfrac{1}{4}$

(E) 4

220. In the figure shown, point R is the midpoint of $\overline{PQ}$, and $\overline{RS}$ has the same length as $\overline{PQ}$. If the length of $\overline{PQ}$ is 6, what is the length of $\overline{PS}$?

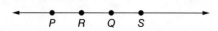

(A) 3

(B) 6

(C) 9

(D) 12

(E) 18

221. Line ℓ has a negative slope, a positive y-intercept, and a positive x-intercept. If line m is parallel to line ℓ, which of the following statements must be true?

    I. Line m has a negative slope.
   II. Line m has a positive y-intercept.
  III. Line m has a positive x-intercept.

(A) I only

(B) II only

(C) III only

(D) II and III only

(E) None of these statements must be true.

222. The line $y = -4x - 9$ passes through point B on the y-axis. What is the value of B?

(A) -15

(B) -9

(C) -5

(D) -4

(E) -1

223. The following table shows selected values on a line $y = mx + b$. What is the value of w?

x	-1	0	1
y	2	w	6

(A) -3

(B) 0

(C) 3

(D) 4

(E) 5

224. The tick marks are equally spaced on the following graph. Which of the following line segments (not shown) would be parallel to $\overline{PQ}$?

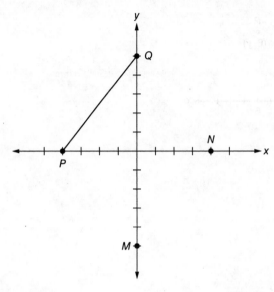

   I. $\overline{QN}$
  II. $\overline{MN}$
 III. $\overline{PM}$

(A) I only
(B) II only
(C) III only
(D) I and II only
(E) I and III only

225. The tick marks are evenly spaced on the figure shown. What is the value of *y*?

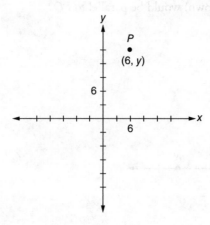

(A) 12

(B) 15

(C) 18

(D) 21

(E) 30

226. Line ℓ passes through the point $(0, 4)$, and line *m* passes through the point $(2, 0)$. If the two lines are parallel and the slope of line ℓ is undefined, what is the shortest distance between a point on ℓ and a point on *m*?

(A) $\sqrt{2}$

(B) 2

(C) 4

(D) $2\sqrt{5}$

(E) $4\sqrt{5}$

227. One can get from Chuck's house to Carly's house by walking three blocks north, two blocks east, and then two more blocks north. In terms of blocks, what is the straight-line distance between Chuck's house and Carly's house?

(A) $3\sqrt{2}$

(B) $\sqrt{7}$

(C) $\sqrt{10}$

(D) $\sqrt{21}$

(E) $\sqrt{29}$

228. A line segment with a slope of −3 starts at the point (0, 6) and ends at the point (x, 0). What is the value of x?

(A) 1

(B) 2

(C) 3

(D) 6

(E) 18

229. A data entry specialist started his day by typing 35 words per minute, steadily, for 4 hours followed by a 1-hour break. Following his break, he steadily typed 20 words per minute for another 4 hours. Which of the following graphs best represents his total words typed (w) in terms of hours (h)?

(A)

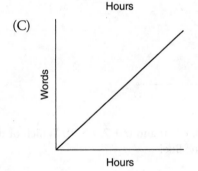

(B)

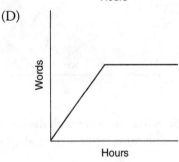

(C)

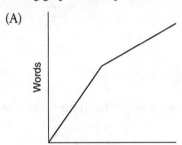

(D)

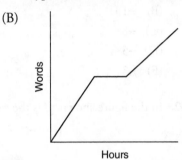

(E)

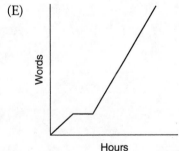

230. Which of the following equations represents a line with a slope of 0?

(A) $x = 5$

(B) $y = 2$

(C) $y = 3x$

(D) $y = 4x - 4$

(E) $y = -10x + 5$

231. The line ℓ is perpendicular to the line $3y + x = 4$ and passes through the point $(0, -5)$. The line $y = t$ intersects ℓ at the point $(-4, t)$. What is the value of t?

(A) -17

(B) -15

(C) -8

(D) -5

(E) -3

232. In the figure shown, B is the midpoint of $\overline{AC}$. What is the value of x?

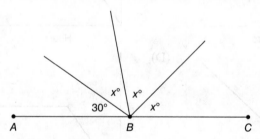

233. A line passes through the points $(t, t + 4)$ and $(t + 7, t + 9)$. Which of the following represents the slope of the line?

(A) $-\dfrac{4}{9}$

(B) $\dfrac{7}{13}$

(C) $\dfrac{5}{7}$

(D) $\dfrac{9}{7}$

(E) $\dfrac{2t + 7}{2t + 13}$

234. In the following figure, ℓ and m are lines such that $\ell \parallel m$. In degrees, what is the value of x?

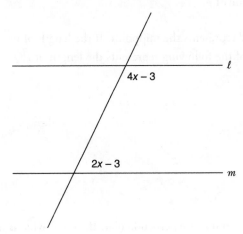

(A) 1
(B) 15
(C) 31
(D) 47
(E) 89

235. Two lines, line 1 and line 2, are perpendicular. If the slope of line 1 is a and the slope of line 2 is b, which of the following is equal to the product of a and b?

(A) -1
(B) 0
(C) 1
(D) a^2
(E) $\dfrac{1}{ab}$

236. A right triangle is formed in the x-y plane by connecting the points $(1, 1)$, $(1, 4)$, and $(0, 1)$. What is the length of the hypotenuse of this triangle?

(A) 2
(B) $\sqrt{3}$
(C) $\sqrt{6}$
(D) $\sqrt{10}$
(E) $\sqrt{26}$

237. The slopes of two parallel lines are p and q, respectively. If the sum of p and q is $\dfrac{7}{8}$, what is the value of p?

238. On a line segment $\overline{PQ}$, M represents the midpoint. If the length of line segment $\overline{QM}$ is x, which of the following represents the length of $\overline{PQ}$ in terms of x?

(A) $\dfrac{x}{2}$

(B) $x - 2$

(C) $x + 2$

(D) $2x$

(E) x^2

239. In the figure shown, lines ℓ and m are perpendicular. If $2x = y$, what is the value of y in degrees?

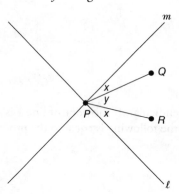

(A) 25

(B) 45

(C) 80

(D) 90

(E) 120

240. In the following figure, the tick marks are evenly spaced. Which of the following represents the equation of a line that passes through line segment $\overline{PQ}$?

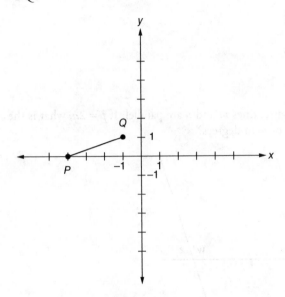

(A) $y = \dfrac{1}{3}x$

(B) $y = 3x$

(C) $y = \dfrac{1}{3}x - 4$

(D) $y = \dfrac{1}{3}x + \dfrac{4}{3}$

(E) $y = 3x - \dfrac{4}{3}$

241. Two lines m and n are parallel and have positive slopes. If the product of the slopes is c, which of the following represents the slope of line m in terms of c?

(A) $\dfrac{c}{2}$

(B) $\sqrt{c}$

(C) $2c$

(D) c^2

(E) This cannot be determined from the information given.

242. What are the coordinates of the point $(-1, 5)$ when it is reflected across the line $y = x$?

(A) $(-1, -5)$

(B) $(-5, -1)$

(C) $(5, -1)$

(D) $(1, -5)$

(E) $(1, 5)$

243. In the following figure, lines m and n are parallel. If $p = 2q$, what is the value of z in terms of w in degrees?

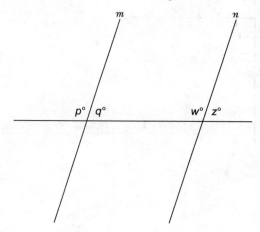

(A) $\dfrac{w}{4}$

(B) $\dfrac{w}{2}$

(C) w

(D) $2w$

(E) $4w$

244. Line ℓ has a positive slope and passes through the origin. Which of the points in the figure shown could the line also pass through?

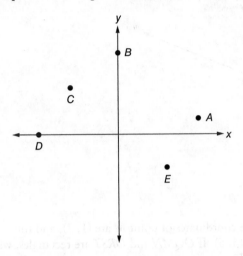

(A) Point A

(B) Point B

(C) Point C

(D) Point D

(E) Point E

245. If the shortest distance from a point P (1, 4) to the x-axis is m and the shortest distance from point P to the y-axis is n, what is the value of $m + n$?

(A) 1

(B) $\sqrt{2}$

(C) $\sqrt{3}$

(D) 4

(E) 5

246. In the following figure, what is the value of $x + y$ in degrees?

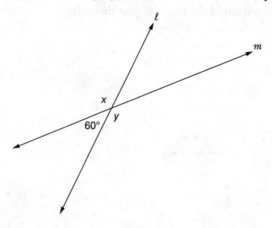

247. In the following figure, the coordinates of point M are (1, 2), and the coordinates of point S are (3, 5). If $OQMN$ and $ORST$ are rectangles, what is the distance from N to T?

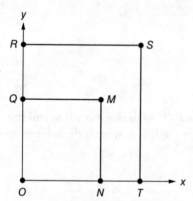

Note: Figure not drawn to scale.

248. If a line in the x-y plane has a slope of one and passes through the point (1, 5), then each of the following points could be on the line EXCEPT

(A) (−10, −6)

(B) (−8, −3)

(C) (−2, 2)

(D) (0, 4)

(E) (2, 6)

249. Line m is parallel to the x-axis and passes through the point $(5, 2)$. What is the y-intercept of m?

(A) −5

(B) −2

(C) 0

(D) 1

(E) 2

250. In the following figure, $\overline{PQ}$, $\overline{QR}$, $\overline{RS}$, $\overline{ST}$, and $\overline{PT}$ are line segments, and all angles except P and T are right angles. What is the length of $\overline{PT}$?

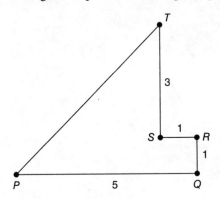

(A) $\sqrt{2}$

(B) 2

(C) 4

(D) $4\sqrt{2}$

(E) 8

251. The points A, B, C, and D lie on a line in alphabetical order such that the length of $\overline{BC}$ is 4 and the length of $\overline{CD}$ is 10. If B is the midpoint of $\overline{AC}$, what is the length of $\overline{AD}$?

252. The slopes of two lines are m and n, respectively. If $m + n = 0$, which of the following statements must be true?

(A) The lines are parallel.

(B) The lines are perpendicular.

(C) The line with slope m is perpendicular to the line with slope n.

(D) The line with slope $-m$ is parallel to the line with slope n.

(E) Both lines pass through the origin.

253. In the following figure, line segment $\overline{PQ}$ has a length of 6. What is the value of $y - x$?

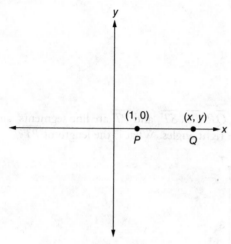

(A) −7

(B) −6

(C) −5

(D) 5

(E) 7

254. Given the y-coordinate of any point on line n, the x-coordinate can be found using the formula $x = -5y + 10$. What is the slope of line n?

(A) −5

(B) −2

(C) $-\dfrac{1}{5}$

(D) $-\dfrac{1}{10}$

(E) 2

255. In the following figure, the slope of $\overline{BC}$ is half the slope of $\overline{AB}$. What is the value of y?

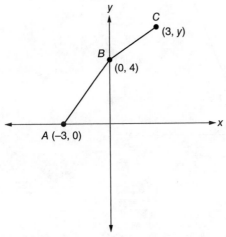

(A) 2
(B) 3
(C) 4
(D) 5
(E) 6

256. The following table represents values of a linear function f for selected values of x. What is the value of a?

f	−1	1	3
x	6	2	a

(A) −6
(B) −2
(C) 1
(D) 3
(E) 4

257. Given line segment $\overline{AB}$ in the following figure, which of the following represents the value of x in terms of y?

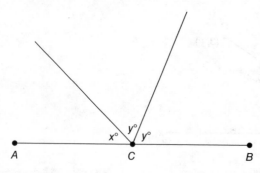

(A) $360 - 2y$

(B) $180 - 2y$

(C) $90 - 2y$

(D) $180y$

(E) $90y$

258. Which of the following is the equation of a line that passes through the origin?

(A) $y + 5x = -2$

(B) $-3y - x = 1$

(C) $2x + 2y = -1$

(D) $3x - 4y = 0$

(E) $x - y = 1$

259. If the rectangle in the figure shown is reflected across the x-axis, what are the coordinates of point *D*?

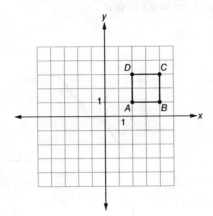

(A) (−2, −3)

(B) (−2, 3)

(C) (2, −3)

(D) (2, 3)

(E) (0, 3)

260. In the following figure, which of the following line segments (not shown) will have a slope of −1?

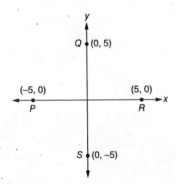

(A) $\overline{PQ}$

(B) $\overline{QR}$

(C) $\overline{RS}$

(D) $\overline{PR}$

(E) $\overline{QS}$

261. A family taking a road trip by car travels at a constant speed with 1-hour breaks every 3 hours. Which of the following graphs could represent the total number of miles the family drives in 12 hours?

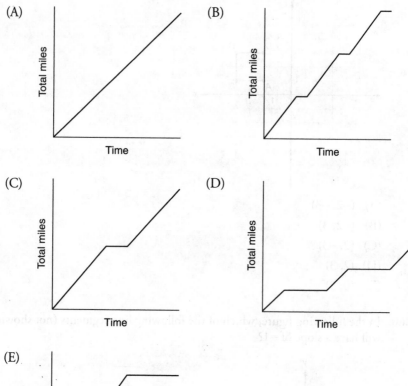

(A)

(B)

(C)

(D)

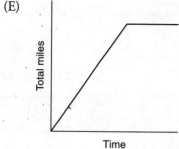

(E)

262. In the following figure, lines ℓ, m, and n share the same point of intersection. If lines m and n are perpendicular, what is the value of x?

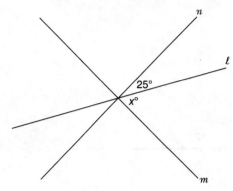

(A) 35
(B) 55
(C) 65
(D) 155
(E) 205

263. If the point $(-7, 19)$ is on a line m with an undefined slope, which of the following points would also be on line m?

(A) $(-7, 0)$
(B) $(0, 19)$
(C) $(0, 0)$
(D) $(0, -7)$
(E) $(19, 0)$

264. What is the area of a circle with a center at $(1, 3)$ and the point $(4, 6)$ on its circumference?

(A) 2π
(B) 3π
(C) 6π
(D) 9π
(E) 18π

265. The tick marks are evenly spaced on the following figure. What is the value of $x + y$?

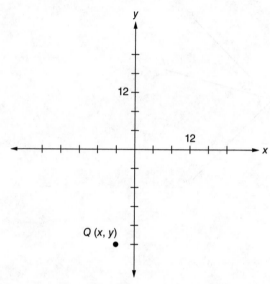

(A) 8
(B) 12
(C) 16
(D) 24
(E) 36

266. What is the slope of a line that passes through the points (x, y) and $(2x, 2y)$ where x and y are nonzero?

(A) $\dfrac{x}{y}$

(B) $\dfrac{y}{x}$

(C) xy

(D) $x - y$

(E) $y - x$

267. If point P is on the x-axis and point Q is on the y-axis, what is the product of their x-coordinates?

(A) −2

(B) −1

(C) 0

(D) 1

(E) This cannot be determined from the information given.

268. In the following figure, lines ℓ and n intersect at point A. What is the sum of x and y in degrees?

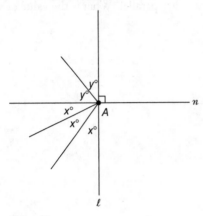

(A) 45

(B) 75

(C) 90

(D) 120

(E) 135

269. Starting from point M, a plane flies due north for 1 hour, due west for 3 hours, and due north again for 2 hours to reach point N. The speed of the plane remains constant at 200 mph for the entire journey. If point M is labeled as the origin with north as the positive direction of the y-axis, what are the coordinates of point N?

(A) (0, 1,200)

(B) (1,200, 0)

(C) (−600, 400)

(D) (600, 200)

(E) (−600, 600)

270. Two points (a, b) and (c, d) lie along the same line k in the x-y plane. If $a - c = 5$ and $b - d = 15$, what is the slope of the line?

(A) −3

(B) $-\dfrac{1}{3}$

(C) 0

(D) $\dfrac{1}{3}$

(E) 3

271. In the following figure, lines m and n are parallel. What is the value of x?

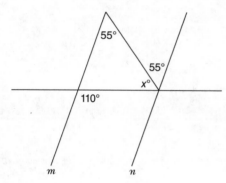

(A) 55

(B) 60

(C) 65

(D) 85

(E) 120

272. Points A, B, C, D, and E are arranged on a line in that order such that D is the midpoint of line segment $\overline{CE}$. If both $\overline{AB}$ and $\overline{CD}$ have a length of 3, then which of the following is a possible value for the length of line segment $\overline{AE}$?

(A) 3

(B) 5

(C) 6

(D) 7

(E) 12

273. In the following figure, the tick marks on the x and y axes are evenly spaced. If the slope of line segment $\overline{PQ}$ (not shown) is m, which of the following line segments has a slope of $\dfrac{m}{2}$?

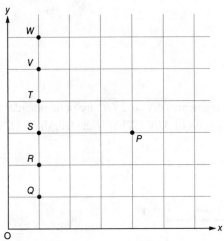

    (A) $\overline{PR}$

    (B) $\overline{PS}$

    (C) $\overline{PT}$

    (D) $\overline{PV}$

    (E) $\overline{PW}$

274. In the following figure, k is a positive integer. What is the approximate minimum possible distance between points A and B?

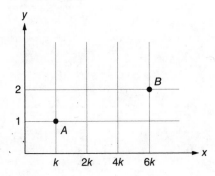

275. Lines p, q, and r intersect at a point C. If the angle between lines p and q is 35° and the angle between lines p and r is 80°, then what is the measure of the angle between lines q and r, in degrees?

(A) 25

(B) 65

(C) 90

(D) 130

(E) 230

276. In the following figure, line segments $\overline{MN}$ and $\overline{NP}$ are perpendicular and the length of $\overline{NP}$ is half the length of $\overline{MN}$. What is the length of $\overline{MP}$?

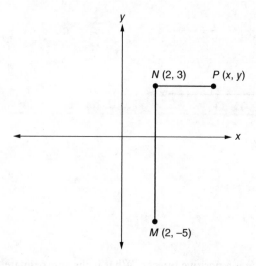

(A) $\sqrt{2}$

(B) $2\sqrt{3}$

(C) $3\sqrt{2}$

(D) $4\sqrt{5}$

(E) $3\sqrt{10}$

277. Given the lines in the following figure, which of the following statements must be true?

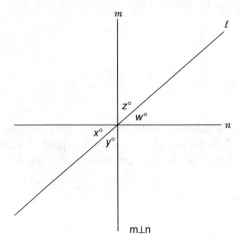

I. $z + x = 90$
II. $z + w = 90$
III. $z = x$

(A) I only
(B) II only
(C) III only
(D) I and II only
(E) I and III only

278. Two lines in the standard x-y plane are parallel. If the points $(-1, 4)$ and $(0, 5)$ are on one of the lines, which of the following could be a point on the other line?

(A) $(-10, -5)$
(B) $(-5, 0)$
(C) $(-2, 6)$
(D) $(3, 8)$
(E) $(7, 12)$

279. If the point P (3, 9) is reflected across the line $y = x$, what are the new coordinates of P?

(A) (9, 3)

(B) (9, 0)

(C) (3, 0)

(D) (−3, −9)

(E) (−9, −3)

280. A particle moves along the path indicated in the following figure, starting at point P and ending at point R. If the particle is moving at a speed of 5 units per second, how many seconds will it take the particle to reach point R?

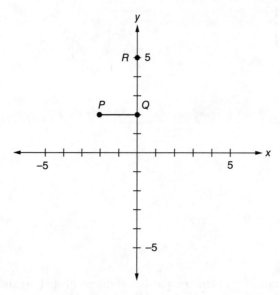

281. What is the minimum distance between the point (−8, 6) and any point on the y-axis?

282. The slope of a line n that passes through the point (−2, −1) is 2. Which of the following points is NOT on line n?

(A) (0, 2)

(B) (1, 5)

(C) (3, 9)

(D) (5, 13)

(E) (10, 23)

283. In the following figure, the tick marks on the x and y axes are evenly spaced. Which of the following are the coordinates of point P?

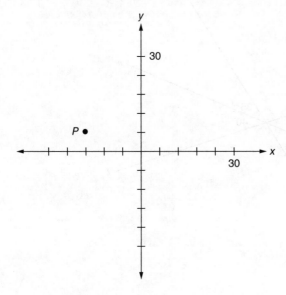

(A) $(-10, -30)$

(B) $(-30, 10)$

(C) $(-18, 6)$

(D) $(-6, -18)$

(E) $(-9, 3)$

284. A line in the standard x-y plane passes through the points $(8, 2)$ and $(-2, 6)$. Which of the following is the equation of a line perpendicular to this line?

(A) $5y + 2x = 20$

(B) $2y - 5x = -12$

(C) $2y + 5x = 14$

(D) $5y - 2x = 5$

(E) $5y - 2x = -15$

285. Using the following figure, what is the value of x, in degrees?

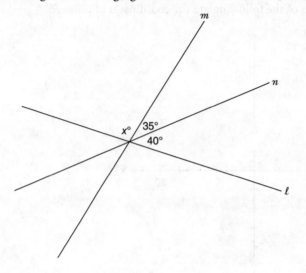

CHAPTER 5

Geometry

286. Triangle *ABC* shown is a right triangle such that ∠*ABC* has a measure of 55°. What is the measure of ∠*BCD*, in degrees?

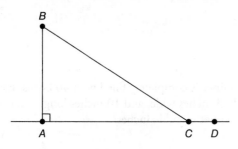

(A) 45

(B) 55

(C) 125

(D) 145

(E) 150

287. The perimeter of a rectangle whose sides have integer lengths is 8 units. In square units, what is the smallest possible area of the rectangle?

288. In square units, what is the area of the following figure?

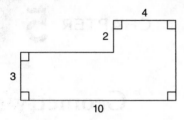

(A) 20

(B) 30

(C) 38

(D) 46

(E) 50

289. A rectangular storage container is completely filled with 40 boxes. Each box measures 2 inches tall, 3 inches wide, and 10 inches long. What is the volume of the storage container in cubic inches?

(A) 100

(B) 400

(C) 640

(D) 1,800

(E) 2,400

290. What is the area of a circle inscribed in a square with sides of length 6?

(A) 6π

(B) 9π

(C) 12π

(D) 18π

(E) 36π

291. In the following figure, points A and B lie on line ℓ such that triangle ABC is an equilateral triangle. What is the value of $x + y$?

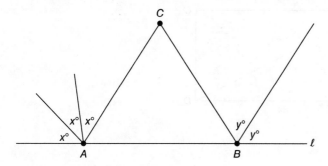

(A) 50

(B) 75

(C) 90

(D) 100

(E) 120

292. In the following figure, square $ABCD$ is inscribed in the circle with center O. If the length of $\overline{AB}$ is 8 and the length of $\overline{PQ}$ is 12, what is the area of the shaded region?

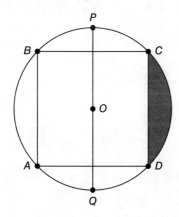

(A) $9\pi - 16$

(B) $12\pi - 16$

(C) $12\pi - 64$

(D) $16\pi - 16$

(E) $36\pi - 64$

293. If the perimeter of rectangle *ABCD* in the following figure is 18, what is the length of $\overline{BD}$?

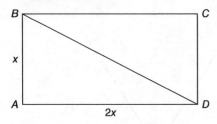

(A) 3

(B) $\sqrt{13}$

(C) $3\sqrt{2}$

(D) $\sqrt{22}$

(E) $3\sqrt{5}$

294. In the following figure, if *a* = 70 and *b* = 80, what is the value of *c*?

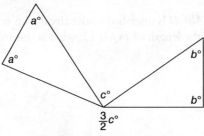

Note: Figure not drawn to scale.

(A) 60

(B) 90

(C) 120

(D) 300

(E) 440

295. A ladder of length 12 feet is placed against a building. If the top of the ladder reaches a height of x feet, which of the following represents the distance from the bottom of the ladder to the building in terms of x?

(A) $\sqrt{x^2 - 144}$

(B) $\sqrt{144 - x^2}$

(C) $\sqrt{12 + x^2}$

(D) $\sqrt{x^2 - 12}$

(E) $x + 12$

296. The area of triangle ABC is twice the area of triangle DEF. The height of triangle ABC is 4, and the height of triangle DEF is 3. If b_1 is the length of the base of triangle ABC and b_2 is the length of the base of triangle DEF, what is the value of $\dfrac{b_1}{b_2}$?

297. In the following figure, triangle ABC is an equilateral triangle and point M is the midpoint of $\overline{AC}$. If the length of side $\overline{BC}$ is 4, what is the perimeter of triangle ABM?

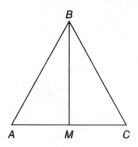

(A) $6 + 2\sqrt{3}$

(B) $6 + 2\sqrt{5}$

(C) $8\sqrt{3}$

(D) $12\sqrt{3}$

(E) $12\sqrt{5}$

298. If the area of the shaded region of the circle in the following figure centered at point O is 90π, what is the length of arc PQ?

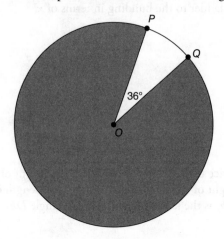

(A) 2π

(B) 9π

(C) 10π

(D) 12π

(E) 18π

299. What is the value of x in the following figure?

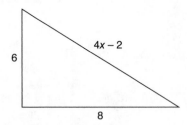

300. Rectangle 1 has sides of length k and $2k$, while rectangle 2 has sides of
length k and $6k$. If k is an integer, how many times larger is the area of
rectangle 2 than the area of rectangle 1?

(A) 3

(B) 4

(C) 6

(D) 8

(E) 10

301. The half circles in the following figure are centered at points *B* and *D*. If the length of line segment $\overline{AB}$ is 4 and the total area of the figure is 40π, what is the length of $\overline{AE}$?

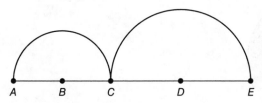

(A) 12

(B) 16

(C) 22

(D) 24

(E) 80

302. In the following figure, triangles *ABC* and *PQR* are equilateral, the length of $\overline{AB}$ is 4, and the length of $\overline{PQ}$ is 2. If *M* is the midpoint of line segments $\overline{AC}$ and $\overline{PR}$, what is the perimeter of the shaded figure?

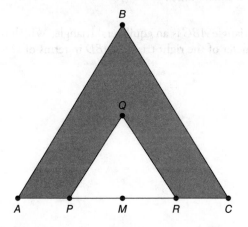

(A) 10

(B) 12

(C) 14

(D) 16

(E) 18

303. The following circle is centered at point A and has an area of 12π. If the total area of the shaded region is 8π, what is the value of $x + y$?

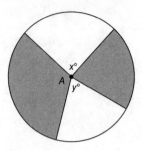

(A) 90

(B) 120

(C) 180

(D) 240

(E) 320

304. The length of a rectangle is six times as large as its width. If its perimeter is 42 units, what is its area in square units?

305. In the following figure, triangle ABC is an equilateral triangle. Which of the following is the perimeter of the right triangle ABD in terms of x?

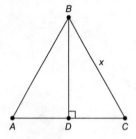

(A) $2x$

(B) $\dfrac{5}{2}x$

(C) $\dfrac{x}{2}\sqrt{3}$

(D) $\dfrac{3+\sqrt{3}}{2}x$

(E) $\dfrac{4+\sqrt{3}}{2}x$

306. Which of the following is the perimeter of the polygon shown outlined by the solid line?

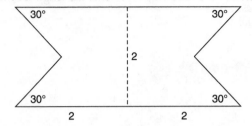

(A) 4

(B) 6

(C) 8

(D) 12

(E) 16

307. In the following figure, triangle *ABC* is an isosceles triangle with *AC* = *BC*. Which of the following is the value of *x*?

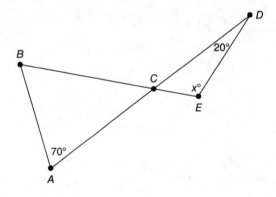

(A) 20

(B) 40

(C) 70

(D) 90

(E) 120

308. A rectangular prism has a height of h and a width of w. If the volume of the prism is $\dfrac{19}{2}$, then which of the following represents the length of the prism in terms of h and w?

(A) $\dfrac{19}{2wh}$

(B) $\dfrac{19wh}{2}$

(C) $wh\sqrt{\dfrac{19}{2}}$

(D) $\dfrac{19}{2} - wh$

(E) $38wh$

309. In the following figure, the diagonals of square $BCDE$ are diameters of the circle centered at point A. If the area of the circle is 32π, then what is the area of square $BCDE$?

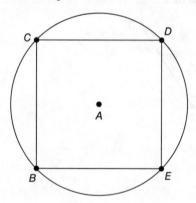

(A) 12
(B) 16
(C) 32
(D) 64
(E) 128

310. One interior angle of a parallelogram has a measure of 80°. If the remaining angles have measures $x°$, $y°$, and $z°$, what is the value of $x + y + z$?

(A) 80

(B) 100

(C) 180

(D) 240

(E) 280

311. It requires 4 gallons of paint to cover 10 square meters of area. If five sides of a cube with a volume of 27 cubic meters are to be painted, how many gallons of paint will be required?

(A) 5

(B) 18

(C) 20

(D) 22

(E) 31

312. In the following figure, points Q and P lie on the circumference of the circle centered at O. If the line segments $\overline{QR}$ and $\overline{PR}$ are tangent to the circle at points Q and P, respectively, what is the value of y?

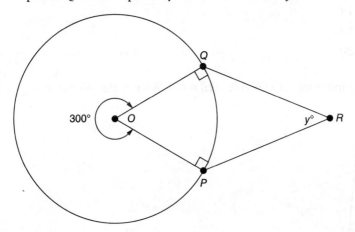

(A) 30

(B) 60

(C) 90

(D) 120

(E) 180

313. If the length of one side of an equilateral triangle is z, which of the following represents the perimeter of the triangle in terms of z?

(A) $\dfrac{z}{2}$

(B) $3z$

(C) $4z$

(D) z^2

(E) z^3

314. In the following figure, $ABCD$ is a rectangle with $AP = QD = 2$. If the area of the shaded region is 24, what is the length of $\overline{BC}$?

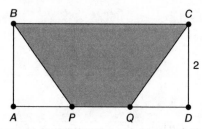

(A) 4

(B) 12

(C) 14

(D) 18

(E) 20

315. In the following triangle ABC, $AB = CB$. What is the value of x?

316. In the following figure, $\overline{AC}$, $\overline{CD}$, and $\overline{DA}$ have the same lengths and $\overline{AC}$ is the diameter of the half circle centered at point B. If the length of $\overline{CD}$ is x, which of the following represents the area of the half circle in terms of x?

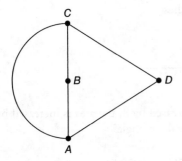

(A) $\dfrac{\pi x^2}{4}$

(B) $\dfrac{\pi x}{2}$

(C) $2x\pi$

(D) $x^2\pi$

(E) $4x^2\pi$

317. In the following figure, ACE and FBD are triangles such that $AB = BF = AF$ and $\angle FBD$ is a right angle. In degrees, what is the measure of $\angle CBD$?

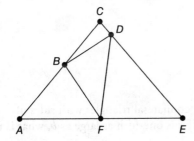

(A) 20

(B) 30

(C) 60

(D) 80

(E) 100

318. A piece of fabric is made of 10 smaller rectangular strips of fabric connected together as in the following figure. Each of the smaller pieces of fabric has the same length and width. If the large piece of fabric has a perimeter of 104 inches and a length of 50 inches, what is the area of one of the 10 smaller pieces in square inches?

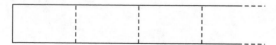

319. When the length of a rectangle is increased by 8, the area is increased by 50%. What is the length of the original rectangle?

320. In the following figure, *ABCH*, *CDGH*, and *GDEF* are congruent squares and the half circles have diameters $\overline{BC}$ and $\overline{DE}$. If $\overline{AB}$ has a length of 2, what is the length of the path outlined by the solid line?

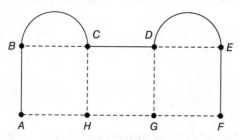

(A) 6π

(B) 8π

(C) 10π

(D) $6 + 2\pi$

(E) $6 + 4\pi$

321. The total perimeter of two separate equilateral triangles with sides of length *a* and *b*, respectively, is 72. If *a* is one-fifth as large as *b*, what is the value of *b*?

322. Using the following figure, what is the value of $x + y$?

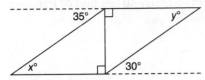

Note: Figure not drawn to scale.

(A) 65

(B) 95

(C) 115

(D) 145

(E) 150

323. What is the area of the shaded region in the following figure?

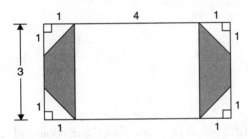

(A) 4

(B) 8

(C) 10

(D) 12

(E) 14

324. A rectangular floor is tiled with square tiles of alternating colors as shown in the following figure. If the room measures 40 feet by 120 feet, what area will be tiled by the lighter color tiles?

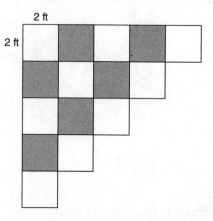

(A) 2,400 square feet

(B) 3,600 square feet

(C) 4,800 square feet

(D) 9,600 square feet

(E) 10,400 square feet

325. In an equilateral triangle ABC, points D, E, and F are the midpoints of $\overline{AB}$, $\overline{BC}$, and $\overline{AC}$, respectively. If $\overline{AD}$ has a length of 2, what is the area of triangle DEF?

(A) $\dfrac{\sqrt{3}}{4}$

(B) $\dfrac{\sqrt{3}}{2}$

(C) $\sqrt{3}$

(D) $4\sqrt{3}$

(E) $6\sqrt{3}$

326. In the following rectangle $ABCD$, the shortest distance between points A and C is d. Which of the following is the value of $x^2 + y^2$ in terms of d?

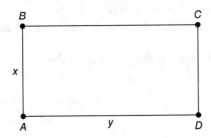

    (A) $\sqrt{d}$

    (B) d

    (C) d^2

    (D) $2d^2$

    (E) $d + \sqrt{d}$

327. The diameter of circle 1 is m, and the diameter of circle 2 is $4m$. How many times larger is the area of circle 2 than the area of circle 1?

    (A) 4

    (B) 8

    (C) 16

    (D) 32

    (E) 64

328. In the following figure, y and z lie along the same line. What is the value of z in terms of x?

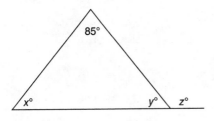

    (A) $85 + x$

    (B) $90 + x$

    (C) $95 + x$

    (D) $120 + x$

    (E) $180 + x$

329. The length of one side of a square is equal to the diameter of a circle. If the area is larger than 1, which of the following statements must be true?

    I. The area of the square is larger than the area of the circle.

    II. The perimeter of the square is smaller than the circumference of the circle.

    III. The radius of the circle is the same as the perimeter of the square.

  (A) I only

  (B) II only

  (C) III only

  (D) I and II only

  (E) I and III only

330. In the following figure, line BD bisects $\angle ABC$ and $b = 65$. What is the value of a?

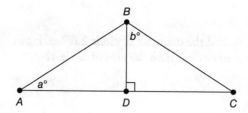

  (A) 15

  (B) 25

  (C) 35

  (D) 45

  (E) 55

331. In the following figure, *ABCE* is a square and *ABD* is a right triangle. What is the value of *x*?

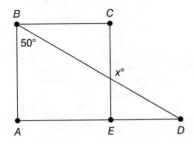

(A) 50
(B) 95
(C) 110
(D) 130
(E) 145

332. In the following figure, *DAB* and *DBC* are triangles such that *DAB* is equilateral. If the perimeter of the figure outlined by the solid line is 18, what is the value of *x* + *y*?

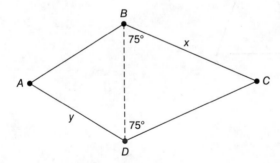

(A) 6
(B) 8
(C) 9
(D) 14
(E) 18

333. Which of the following represents the area of a right triangle whose interior angles measure 45°, 45°, and 90° and whose hypotenuse has a length of $3\sqrt{2}$?

(A) $\dfrac{1}{2}$

(B) $\dfrac{3}{2}$

(C) $\dfrac{3\sqrt{2}}{2}$

(D) $\dfrac{9}{2}$

(E) $9\sqrt{2}$

334. In the following triangles, $AB = BC$ and $CD = DE$. If $\angle BAC = \angle DEC = 65°$, then $\angle BCD =$

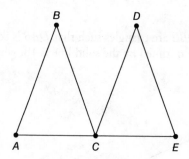

(A) 50°

(B) 65°

(C) 70°

(D) 95°

(E) 115°

335. The base of a 10-meter-tall cylindrical container is a circle with a radius of 4 meters. If the container is completely filled, how many cubic meters of water can it hold?

(A) 40π

(B) 80π

(C) 160π

(D) 210π

(E) 400π

336. The following figure consists of two concentric circles centered at point A with radii of 5 and 9, respectively. What is the area of the shaded region?

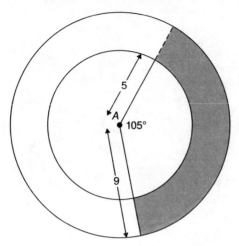

(A) $\dfrac{\pi}{3}$

(B) $\dfrac{4\pi}{3}$

(C) $\dfrac{14\pi}{3}$

(D) $\dfrac{49\pi}{3}$

(E) $\dfrac{56\pi}{3}$

337. In the following figure, each square in the grid has sides of length 1. What is the area of the quadrilateral $ABCD$?

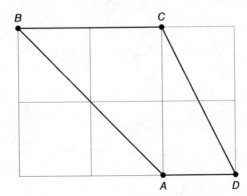

338. If triangle *ABC* in the following figure is an equilateral triangle, what is its perimeter?

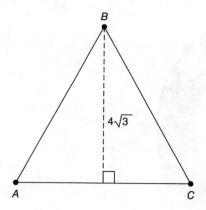

(A) 4

(B) 16

(C) 24

(D) $12\sqrt{3}$

(E) $16\sqrt{3}$

339. The diagonal of a square has a length of $8\sqrt{2}$. What is the area of the square?

340. In the following figure, *ABCD* is a parallelogram and *DCE* is a triangle. If $y = 55$, what is the value of *x*?

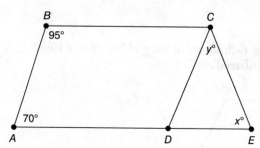

(A) 40

(B) 55

(C) 70

(D) 85

(E) 95

341. In the following figure, *ABCD* is a square and *DEFG* is a rectangle. If
AD = *DE* and *BC* = 4, what would be the length of a line between points
A and *G*?

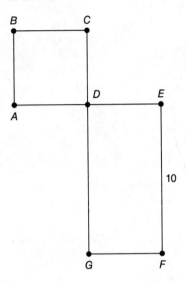

(A) $4\sqrt{13}$

(B) $2\sqrt{21}$

(C) $\sqrt{19}$

(D) $\sqrt{58}$

(E) $2\sqrt{29}$

342. In the following figure, AOB is a segment of the circle centered at O with a radius of 5. If the angle AOB has a measure of 40 degrees, what is the perimeter of the segment AOB outlined with a solid line?

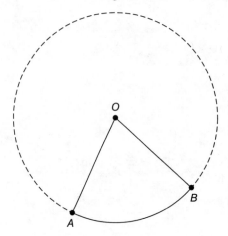

(A) $5 + \dfrac{\pi}{9}$

(B) $5 + \dfrac{10\pi}{9}$

(C) $5 + \dfrac{25\pi}{9}$

(D) $10 + \dfrac{10\pi}{9}$

(E) $10 + \dfrac{25\pi}{9}$

343. Which of the following represents the perimeter of a square that has an area of x^2?

(A) $\dfrac{1}{2}x$

(B) x

(C) $2x$

(D) $3x$

(E) $4x$

344. In the following figure, *ABCD* is a single face of a cube, and the length of the diagonal $\overline{BD}$ is *x*. Which of the following represents the volume of the cube in terms of *x*?

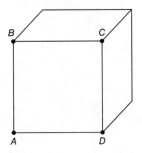

(A) $\dfrac{x^3\sqrt{2}}{4}$

(B) $\dfrac{x^3\sqrt{2}}{2}$

(C) $x^2\sqrt{2}$

(D) $\dfrac{x\sqrt{2}}{4}$

(E) $x\sqrt{2}$

345. When the radius of a circle is halved, the area of the new circle is 16π. What is the radius of the original circle?

346. The circumference of circle *A* is three times as large as the circumference of circle *B*. If the radius of circle *A* is *r*, which of the following represents the radius of circle *B* in terms of *r*?

(A) $\dfrac{r}{6}$

(B) $\dfrac{r}{3}$

(C) r

(D) $3r$

(E) $6r$

347. The diagonals of a square *ABCD* are $\overline{BD}$ and $\overline{CA}$. If the area of triangle *ABD* is 8, what is the perimeter of *ABCD*?

348. The areas of triangle *ABE* and triangle *ECD* in the following figure are 21 and 30, respectively. If *E* is the midpoint of line segment $\overline{AD}$, what is the value of *x*?

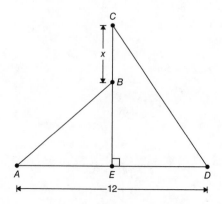

(A) 3

(B) 5

(C) 9

(D) 7

(E) 10

349. In the following figure, *ABD* is a quarter circle with a radius of 10. What is the area of the shaded region?

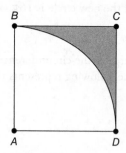

(A) 10π

(B) $10 - 4\pi$

(C) $20 - 25\pi$

(D) $100 - 25\pi$

(E) $100 - 100\pi$

350. In the following figure, *ABDE* is a square and *C* is the midpoint of $\overline{BD}$. If *BC* = 2, what is the area of triangle *ACE*?

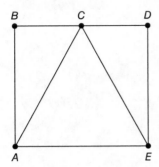

(A) 6

(B) 8

(C) 12

(D) 16

(E) 20

351. If the points *A*, *B*, *C*, *D*, *E*, and *F* form a hexagon and each point is connected to every other point by a line segment, how many line segments will contain point *A*?

(A) 2

(B) 4

(C) 5

(D) 6

(E) 8

352. What is the volume of a cube with a surface area of 294?

353. What is the area of the largest right triangle that can be drawn completely within a rectangle with sides of length 3 and 8?

(A) 11

(B) 12

(C) 18

(D) 20

(E) 24

354. The following circle is centered at point A, and the shaded region has an area of 3π. What is the diameter of the circle?

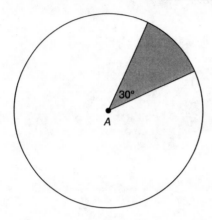

(A) 4

(B) 6

(C) 12

(D) 24

(E) 36

355. The circumference of a circle is C and the perimeter of a square is P such that $P = \dfrac{C}{\pi}$. If the area of the circle is A_c and the area of the square is A_S, then $A_S =$

(A) A_c

(B) $\dfrac{A_c}{\pi}$

(C) $\dfrac{A_c}{2\pi}$

(D) $\dfrac{A_c}{3\pi}$

(E) $\dfrac{A_c}{4\pi}$

356. Two rectangular prisms A and B have the same width and height. If the length of prism A is a third of that of prism B, then the ratio of the volume of A to the volume of B is

(A) $1:3$

(B) $1:6$

(C) $1:9$

(D) $1:12$

(E) $1:27$

357. In the following figure, if GCF is an equilateral triangle, then $x + y =$

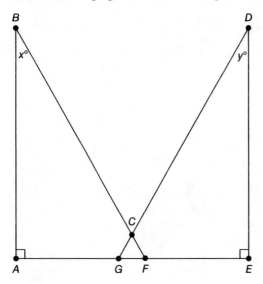

(A) 30

(B) 60

(C) 120

(D) 130

(E) 160

358. In the following figure, the half circles centered at points B and D have radii of x and $2x$, respectively. Which of the following represents the length of the path denoted by the solid line in terms of x?

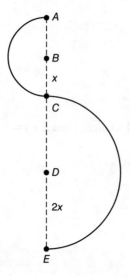

(A) $2\pi x$

(B) $3\pi x$

(C) $4\pi x$

(D) $6\pi x$

(E) $8\pi x$

CHAPTER 6

Proportions

359. In a bag containing only two colors of marbles, the ratio of red marbles to green marbles is 2 to 3. If there are 800 marbles in the bag, how many are red?

(A) 270

(B) 320

(C) 480

(D) 530

(E) 660

360. In a club with x members, 75% regularly attend meetings, and 20% of these members are considered senior members. In terms of x, which of the following represents the number of members who regularly attend meetings that are considered senior members?

(A) $0.15x$

(B) $0.25x$

(C) $0.35x$

(D) $0.75x$

(E) $0.95x$

361. If x is a positive number, which of the following is equivalent to $x\%$ of 125?

(A) $\dfrac{5x}{4}$

(B) $\dfrac{25x}{4}$

(C) $\dfrac{5}{4x}$

(D) $\dfrac{5}{8x}$

(E) $\dfrac{125}{x}$

362. A vehicle travels at a constant speed of m miles per hour. Which of the following represents the distance the vehicle will cover in 15 minutes in terms of m?

(A) $\dfrac{m}{4}$

(B) $\dfrac{m}{2}$

(C) m

(D) $2m$

(E) $4m$

363. Rectangles A and B are similar such that the length of A is 5 while the length of B is 25. If the width of A is w, which of the following represents the width of B in terms of w?

(A) $\dfrac{w}{5}$

(B) $w - 5$

(C) $w + 5$

(D) $5w$

(E) w^5

364. Suppose y varies directly as x and $y = c^2$ when $x = \dfrac{c}{2}$ for some nonzero constant c. In terms of c, what is the value of y when $x = 5$?

(A) $\dfrac{c^2}{10}$

(B) $\dfrac{c}{5}$

(C) $5c$

(D) $10c$

(E) $5c^2$

365. If x and y are real numbers, which of the following is equivalent to 45% of $6x + 10y$?

(A) $\dfrac{x+y}{100}$

(B) $\dfrac{9x+9y}{2}$

(C) $\dfrac{27x+45y}{10}$

(D) $\dfrac{54x+90y}{2}$

(E) $\dfrac{90x+9y}{5}$

366. The price of a single piece of furniture was increased by 25%. After the increase, five pieces of the furniture were sold for a total of $675. To the nearest cent, what was the original price of a single piece of this type of furniture?

(A) $101.25

(B) $108.00

(C) $126.56

(D) $135.00

(E) $157.22

367. At the end of a season, a baseball team had won its home games at a ratio of 3 to 1. If the team played a total of 80 games and 40% were home games, how many home games did it lose?

(A) 3

(B) 8

(C) 12

(D) 24

(E) 29

368. If $\dfrac{a}{b} = \dfrac{3}{11}$, then $\dfrac{a+b}{b} =$

(A) $\dfrac{8}{11}$

(B) $\dfrac{14}{11}$

(C) 3

(D) 4

(E) 11

369. Suppose m varies inversely as n. If when $m = 5$, $n = 1$, then when $n = x$, $m =$

(A) $\dfrac{x}{6}$

(B) $\dfrac{x}{5}$

(C) $5x$

(D) $6x$

(E) $11x$

370. In a set containing n numbers, 40% are divisible by a positive integer k. Which of the following represents the fraction of numbers in the set that have a nonzero remainder when divided by k?

(A) $\dfrac{1}{5}$

(B) $\dfrac{2}{5}$

(C) $\dfrac{3}{5}$

(D) $\dfrac{4}{5}$

(E) This cannot be determined from the information given.

371. When a number x is increased by 40%, the resulting value is 92. If x is decreased by 10%, then the resulting value is

(A) $\dfrac{23}{10}$

(B) $\dfrac{230}{7}$

(C) $\dfrac{184}{5}$

(D) $\dfrac{414}{7}$

(E) $\dfrac{460}{7}$

372. A special set of 200 cards contains blue and green cards only. If the set contains 54 more blue cards than green cards, then what percentage of the deck is made up of green cards?

(A) 27%

(B) 36.5%

(C) 41.2%

(D) 63.5%

(E) 99.7%

373. In a meeting of junior and senior high school students, the ratio of juniors to seniors is 1 : 3. Each of the following could be the total number of students at the meeting EXCEPT

(A) 16

(B) 52

(C) 58

(D) 60

(E) 76

374. Exactly two years ago, a student purchased 10 shares of a stock. In the first year, the value increased by 3%. In the second year, the price increased by another 5%. If the student originally paid $140.60 for the 10 shares, then what is the current price of a single share to the nearest cent?

375. A recipe requires that the amount of flour and sugar used follow a ratio of $2 : 3$. If $1\frac{1}{4}$ cups of flour are used, how many cups of sugar should be used?

376. If $\frac{1}{4}\%$ of x is 19, then $x =$

(A) 0.76

(B) 7.6

(C) 76

(D) 760

(E) 7,600

377. If a is directly proportional to b and $a = 18$ when $b = 3$, then when $b = \frac{1}{3}$, $a =$

(A) $\frac{1}{18}$

(B) 2

(C) 15

(D) $\frac{46}{3}$

(E) 21

378. Suppose for two variables x and y that when $x = \sqrt{2}$, $y = 4$. If y is directly proportional to x, then which of the following equations describes their relationship?

(A) $y = \frac{\sqrt{2}}{4}x$

(B) $y = \frac{\sqrt{2}}{2}x$

(C) $y = 2x\sqrt{2}$

(D) $y = 4x\sqrt{2}$

(E) $y = 8x\sqrt{2}$

379. The length of a sailboat is 60 feet. If a scale model of this boat is to be built such that the ratio of the model to the actual sailboat is 1 : 80, what will the length of the model be, in feet?

380. During a sale, customers can purchase one pound of apples at a 15% discount. Customers may also use a coupon to receive an additional 2% off the sale price. If the price of a pound of apples before the sale was x, which of the following represents the price during the sale if the coupon is used?

(A) $\dfrac{3x}{1,000}$

(B) $\dfrac{13x}{1,000}$

(C) $\dfrac{17x}{1,000}$

(D) $\dfrac{147x}{1,000}$

(E) $\dfrac{833x}{1,000}$

381. An employee is able to input 48 lines of data every 40 minutes. If he is asked to input lines of data for 210 minutes, how many complete lines of data will he be able to input?

(A) 166

(B) 175

(C) 218

(D) 240

(E) 252

382. The ratio of the height of triangle A to the height of triangle B is 1 : 3. If the triangles are similar, what is the ratio of the area of triangle A to the area of triangle B?

(A) 1 : 3

(B) 1 : 6

(C) 1 : 9

(D) 1 : 12

(E) This cannot be determined from the information given.

383. If x is greater than $\dfrac{1}{8}$% of 2,115, then which of the following is the smallest possible integer value of x?

(A) 2

(B) 3

(C) 8

(D) 26

(E) 265

384. If Bobby can run 3 miles in 20 minutes and Aiden can run 3 miles in 25 minutes, what is the difference in the number of miles they can run in 100 minutes?

(A) 0

(B) 3

(C) 12

(D) 15

(E) 18

385. If the ratio of x to y is 2 : 7, which of the following equations must be true?

(A) $x - y = 5$

(B) $xy = 14$

(C) $2x = 7y$

(D) $7x = 2y$

(E) $x + y = 9$

386. Which of the following represents $\dfrac{a}{b}$% of 100?

(A) $\dfrac{a}{b}$

(B) $\dfrac{100a}{b}$

(C) $\dfrac{a}{100b}$

(D) $\dfrac{1{,}000a}{b}$

(E) $\dfrac{a}{1{,}000b}$

387. A customer purchases items from a grocery store totaling $34.86. If he uses a loyalty card that provides a discount and must only pay $30.19, then what percentage discount did he receive?

388. Tutor A charges a student $90 for 3 hours of tutoring, while Tutor B charges a student $40 for 1 hour of tutoring. Which of the following is the ratio of the hourly rate for Tutor A to the hourly rate of Tutor B?

(A) $1:1$

(B) $1:2$

(C) $2:3$

(D) $1:4$

(E) $3:4$

389. If m varies directly as n, and $m = 6a$ when $n = a$, then what is the value of m when $n = 3$?

390. If 80% of x is 480, then $x =$

391. Gina rides her bike to the grocery store from her house at an average speed of 12 mph and returns along the same route at an average speed of 18 mph. If her total travel time was 45 minutes, what is the total round-trip distance, in miles, from her house to the grocery store and back?

392. A restaurant stocks dinner and dessert plates in a ratio of $5:3$. If the restaurant stocks a total of n plates for dinner and dessert, which of the following represents the number of dinner plates?

(A) $\dfrac{5n}{8}$

(B) $\dfrac{5n}{3}$

(C) $2n$

(D) $3n$

(E) $5n$

393. If x is a positive number, what percentage of $5x$ is x?

  (A) 2%

  (B) 5%

  (C) 20%

  (D) 25%

  (E) 50%

394. If b varies directly as $a^2 + 1$, and $b = 10$ when $a = 2$, then when a = 5, what is b?

395. In a right triangle A, the hypotenuse has a length of 8 and the smallest interior angle is 30 degrees. In another right triangle B, the smallest interior angle is also 30 degrees but the hypotenuse has a length of 2. What is the ratio of the area of triangle A to the area of triangle B?

  (A) 2 : 1

  (B) 4 : 1

  (C) 16 : 1

  (D) 32 : 1

  (E) This cannot be determined from the information given.

396. In dollars, which of the following represents the price of an $\$m$ item after a 10% discount?

  (A) $\dfrac{1}{10}m$

  (B) $\dfrac{1}{5}m$

  (C) $\dfrac{4}{5}m$

  (D) $\dfrac{9}{10}m$

  (E) $\dfrac{11}{10}m$

397. If x and y are positive numbers, which of the following is equivalent to $\frac{1}{x}\%$ of $\frac{25}{y}$?

(A) $\dfrac{1}{100xy}$

(B) $\dfrac{1}{4xy}$

(C) $\dfrac{2}{5xy}$

(D) $\dfrac{25}{xy}$

(E) $\dfrac{100}{xy}$

398. Tanya purchased a video game for $45.99. If her purchase included a 20% discount, what was the original price of the game, in dollars?

399. If the value of x decreases by 12%, its value is a. If the original value of x increases by 10%, its value is b. In terms of x, what is the value of $a - b$?

(A) $-0.22x$

(B) $-0.02x$

(C) $0.98x$

(D) $x - 0.02$

(E) $x + 0.98$

400. If 0.06% of x is 6, then $x =$

(A) 10

(B) 100

(C) 1,000

(D) 10,000

(E) 100,000

401. A factory is able to produce 2 large machines every 3 days. How many complete machines can be completed by the factory in 20 days?

(A) 6

(B) 7

(C) 12

(D) 13

(E) 14

402. If $c\%$ of 18 is $c - 5$, then what is c?

403. If the length of a single side of a cube is x, what is the ratio of the area of a single face of the cube to the volume of the cube?

(A) $1 : x$

(B) $1 : x^2$

(C) $1 : x^3$

(D) $1 : x^4$

(E) $1 : x^5$

404. If the ratio of m to n is $2 : 9$, then the ratio of $18m$ to n is

(A) $4 : 1$

(B) $9 : 1$

(C) $12 : 1$

(D) $16 : 1$

(E) $36 : 1$

405. In a bag of marbles, there are 15% more red marbles than blue marbles. If the bag contains only these two colors of marbles, then which of the following is a possible value for the total number of marbles in the bag?

(A) 80

(B) 165

(C) 245

(D) 310

(E) 430

406. If t is inversely proportional to r, and $t = 6$ when $r = 2$, then when $r = \dfrac{1}{4}$, what is t?

407. If the difference between 25% of x and 20% of x is 14, then what is the value of x?

408. The ratio of Frank's hourly pay to Rich's hourly pay is 5 : 6. If after two hours of work, Frank and Rich are paid a total of $66, what is Rich's hourly pay?
(A) $12
(B) $15
(C) $18
(D) $22
(E) $40

409. Suppose y varies inversely as x and when $x = 12n$, $y = \dfrac{1}{3}n$ for some non-zero n. In terms of n, what is the value of y when $x = 2n$?
(A) $\dfrac{n}{4}$
(B) $\dfrac{n}{2}$
(C) $2n$
(D) $4n$
(E) $4n^2$

410. If x and y are positive numbers such that $x\%$ of y is a, then in terms of a, what is $y\%$ of x?
(A) $\dfrac{a}{100}$
(B) $\dfrac{a}{50}$
(C) $\dfrac{a}{10}$
(D) a
(E) $100a$

411. The following table represents the enrollment in a statistics course at a small college. To the nearest tenth of a percent, what has been the percentage increase in enrollment from 2010 to 2013?

Year	Enrollment
2010	135
2011	130
2012	140
2013	155

(A) 1.2%

(B) 3.7%

(C) 11.1%

(D) 14.8%

(E) 87.1%

412. A scale model of a square-shaped garden is to be built such that each foot of length in the scale model represents 100 feet in the actual garden. If the garden has an area of 62,500 square feet, what will be the area of the scale model, in square feet?

(A) 5.5

(B) 6.25

(C) 550

(D) 625

(E) 1,025

413. At a construction site, x nails are used every 6 hours. In terms of x, how many nails are used in 20 hours?

(A) $\dfrac{10x}{3}$

(B) $\dfrac{20x}{3}$

(C) $\dfrac{26x}{3}$

(D) $20x$

(E) $26x$

414. At a retail establishment, the number of employees required on shift is directly proportional to the number of people entering the building during the shift. If the establishment required 20 employees during a shift when 850 people entered the building, how many employees will be required when it is estimated that 340 customers enter the building during their shift?

(A) 4

(B) 8

(C) 14

(D) 28

(E) 50

415. For every five $10 bills, a wallet contains fifteen $1 bills. Which of the following is the ratio of $10 bills to $1 bills in the wallet?

(A) 1 : 2

(B) 1 : 3

(C) 10 : 1

(D) 10 : 3

(E) 15 : 1

416. In a group of first graders, x say that green is their favorite color. When asked an hour later, three of them change their minds and decide that green is no longer their favorite color. If there are y first graders in the group, which of the following represents the percentage that now say green is their favorite color?

(A) $100\left(\dfrac{x}{y}-3\right)\%$

(B) $100\left(\dfrac{x}{y}+3\right)\%$

(C) $\dfrac{100(x-3)}{y}\%$

(D) $\dfrac{100x}{y+3}\%$

(E) $\dfrac{100(x-3)}{y+3}\%$

417. If x and y are positive numbers, which of the following represents $(x + y)\%$ of $\dfrac{50}{x^2 + 2xy + y^2}$?

(A) $\dfrac{1}{2}(x + y)$

(B) $2(x + y)$

(C) $\dfrac{1}{2(x + y)}$

(D) $\dfrac{2(x + y)}{x - y}$

(E) $\dfrac{x + y}{2(x - y)}$

418. If 64% of students in a class earn a grade of B or higher, what fraction of students earn a grade of C or lower?

(A) $\dfrac{4}{25}$

(B) $\dfrac{9}{25}$

(C) $\dfrac{12}{25}$

(D) $\dfrac{16}{25}$

(E) $\dfrac{19}{25}$

419. If the ratio of a to b is 3 : 17, then what is the value of b when $a = \dfrac{13}{2}$?

420. The value of an antique decreases by 8% one year and by 2% the next. After this, to the nearest tenth of a percent, the antique is worth what percentage of its original value?

(A) 1.9%

(B) 10.0%

(C) 16.0%

(D) 18.4%

(E) 90.2%

421. A club saw an $x\%$ increase in the number of members over a one-month period where $5 < x < 10$. If before the increase there were 250 members, which of the following is a possible value for the number of members after the increase?

(A) 262

(B) 270

(C) 275

(D) 286

(E) 294

422. If 15% of a number is 35, then 3% of the number is

(A) 3

(B) 4

(C) 5

(D) 6

(E) 7

423. The price of item A is $\$m$, and the price of item B is $\$n$. If item A goes on sale for 10% off and item B goes on sale for 20% off, which of the following represents the cost of buying both items while they are on sale, in dollars?

(A) $\dfrac{m+n}{5}$

(B) $\dfrac{3m+2n}{10}$

(C) $\dfrac{9m+8n}{10}$

(D) $10m + 20n$

(E) $30(m + n)$

424. If x is 5% of $\dfrac{1}{4}$, then $x =$

(A) $\dfrac{1}{80}$

(B) $\dfrac{1}{60}$

(C) $\dfrac{1}{40}$

(D) $\dfrac{1}{20}$

(E) $\dfrac{1}{2}$

425. A clothing store sells a type of jacket in three different sizes: small, medium, and large. Of the store's entire stock of this jacket, 10% are small and 40% are medium. If there are 170 jackets in stock, how many are large?

426. If $\frac{1}{8}y = x$, and both are nonzero, then what percent of y is x?

    (A) 1.25%

    (B) 8%

    (C) 12.5%

    (D) 125%

    (E) 800%

427. The ratio of the numbers x, y, and z is 1 to 3 to 5. If $y = x + 1$, what is the value of z?

428. A particle's path and speed can be represented in the x-y coordinate plane by movement along the x-axis at a rate of 4 units every 20 minutes. If the start of the particle's path is represented by the origin and it moves in the positive direction, at which of the following points is the particle located after 50 minutes?

    (A) (3, 0)

    (B) (8, 0)

    (C) (10, 0)

    (D) (20, 0)

    (E) (24, 0)

CHAPTER 7

Functions

429. Which of the following functions has three distinct zeros?

(A) x^2

(B) x^3

(C) $x(x-4)^2$

(D) $x(x+4)(x-4)$

(E) $(x-1)(x+1)^2$

430. What is the maximum y value reached by the graph of $f(x) = -x^2 - 5$?

(A) -5

(B) -4

(C) -2

(D) 0

(E) 1

431. If $a^3(a^2 - 1) = 0$, then which of the following is a possible value of a?

(A) -8

(B) -2

(C) 0

(D) 2

(E) 8

432. If $f(x) = x^2 - x$, then which of the following represents $f(c+1)$?

(A) $c^2 - 1$

(B) $c^2 + 1$

(C) $c^2 + c$

(D) $c^2 + c - 1$

(E) $c^2 - c - 1$

433. What is the largest value of x that makes the equation $3x^2 - 16x = -5$ true?

434. If $g(x) = \dfrac{x-6}{x^2}$ for all nonzero x, then $g(-1) =$

(A) -7

(B) -6

(C) -5

(D) 5

(E) 6

435. If $f(x) = x + 5$, then $f\left(\dfrac{1}{8}k + 6\right) =$

(A) $\dfrac{15}{4}k$

(B) $\dfrac{15}{4}k + 11$

(C) $\dfrac{5}{8}k + 30$

(D) $\dfrac{1}{8}k + 30$

(E) $\dfrac{1}{8}k + 11$

436. If the graph of $f(x)$ is pictured as shown, which of the following would be the graph of $f(x-2)$?

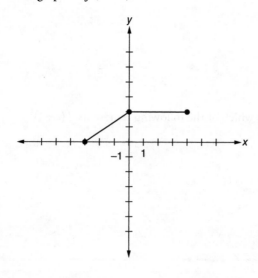

(A)

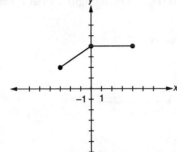

(B)

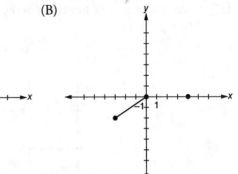

(C)

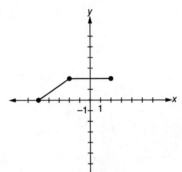

(D)

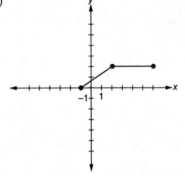

(E)

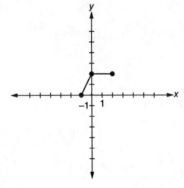

437. Given the graph of a function f in the following figure, what is the value of $f(1) + f(3)$?

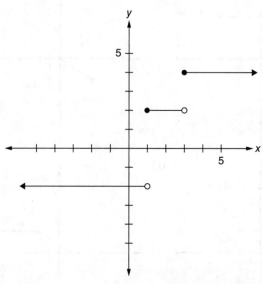

(A) 2

(B) 3

(C) 4

(D) 5

(E) 6

438. Given the graph of a function $f(x) = ax^2 + bx + c$ in the following figure, which of the following statements must be true?

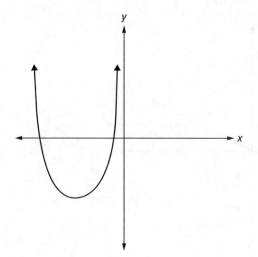

   I. $a > 0$
  II. $b \neq 0$
 III. $c = 0$

(A) I only
(B) II only
(C) III only
(D) I and II only
(E) I and III only

439. Given the graph of the function $g(x)$ in the following figure, for which values of x is $g(x) > 0$?

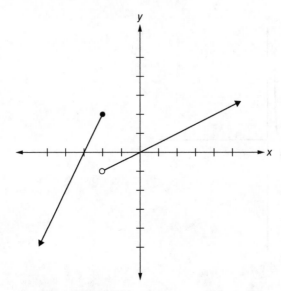

(A) $x \geq -3$ only
(B) $x \geq -2$ only
(C) $x \geq 0$ only
(D) $-3 \leq x \leq -2$ only
(E) $-3 \leq x \leq -2$ and $x \geq 0$

440. If the graph of a quadratic function $f(x) = ax^2 + bx + c$ has x-intercepts at $(4, 0)$ and $(-3, 0)$, then $b =$
(A) -12
(B) -1
(C) 0
(D) 1
(E) 5

441. Given the function $f(x) = x - 8$, if $n > 2$, then $f(n)$ must be greater than
(A) -16
(B) -14
(C) -12
(D) -8
(E) -6

442. If $g(x) = \dfrac{x+1}{x}$ for all nonzero x and $g(k+1) = 3$, then which of the following is the value of k?

(A) $-\dfrac{4}{3}$

(B) $-\dfrac{1}{2}$

(C) $-\dfrac{1}{3}$

(D) $-\dfrac{1}{4}$

(E) $\dfrac{1}{2}$

443. A function $k(x)$ is defined such that if x is even, $k(x)$ is 4, and if x is odd, $k(x)$ is 6. What is the value of $k(1) + k(2)$?

(A) 2

(B) 4

(C) 6

(D) 10

(E) 24

444. Given the graphs of functions f and g shown, which of the following is an equation representing $g(x)$ in terms of $f(x)$?

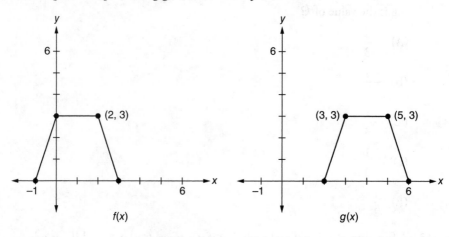

(A) $g(x) = f(x-3)$

(B) $g(x) = f(x+3)$

(C) $g(x) = f(x)-3$

(D) $g(x) = f(x)+3$

(E) $g(x) = 3f(x)$

445. The graph of a quadratic function does not cross the x-axis and has a maximum at the point $(0, -4)$. Which of the following is a possible equation for the described function?

(A) $-\dfrac{3}{4}x^2 - 4$

(B) $-\dfrac{1}{2}x^2 + 4$

(C) $4x^2 - 4$

(D) $x^2 + 4$

(E) $x^2 - 4$

446. Given the following graph of the function $f(x)$, if $f(x) > 1$ and x is a positive integer, what is the smallest possible value of x?

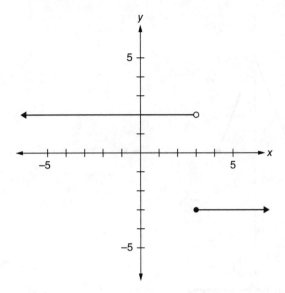

447. If $f(x) = \dfrac{1}{3}x + 5$ and $g(x) = f(x) - 1$, then the slope of the graph of $g(x)$ must be

(A) -5

(B) -3

(C) $\dfrac{1}{5}$

(D) $\dfrac{1}{4}$

(E) $\dfrac{1}{3}$

448. If points A and C of triangle ABC in the following figure lie on the graph of $h(x) = x^2 - 8$, then which of the following is the area of triangle ABC?

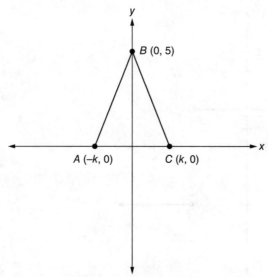

Note: Figure not drawn to scale.

(A) $\sqrt{2}$

(B) $4\sqrt{2}$

(C) $8\sqrt{2}$

(D) $10\sqrt{2}$

(E) $20\sqrt{2}$

449. If $f(n) = n^4 - 4n$, then $f(-1) =$

(A) -8

(B) 4

(C) 5

(D) 8

(E) 9

450. If the point $(-1, 5)$ is on the graph of a function $g(x)$, and $h(x) = g(x) - k$ for some constant k, then which of the following points must be on the graph of $h(x)$?

(A) $(-k, 5k)$

(B) $(-1, 5 - k)$

(C) $(k - 1, 5)$

(D) $(-1 - k, 5)$

(E) $(-1, 5 + k)$

451. The graphs of $f(x) = x^2 + 1$ and $g(x) = kx^2$ intersect at the point $\left(\dfrac{\sqrt{2}}{2}, n \right)$ for some constant n. What is the value of k?

(A) 1

(B) 2

(C) 3

(D) 4

(E) This cannot be determined from the information given.

452. If $f(x) = 3x^2 - 4$ and $g(x) = \dfrac{1}{2} f(x) + 4$, then what is the value of $g(4)$?

(A) 18

(B) 20

(C) 26

(D) 28

(E) 48

453. The number of lines of code $c(h)$ a programmer wrote per hour h over a 12-hour period can be described by the function $c(h) = -h^2 + 12h$ for $0 \le h \le 12$. What was the maximum number of lines of code the programmer wrote during any one hour?

(A) 2

(B) 6

(C) 8

(D) 24

(E) 36

454. If the value of a car y years after purchase can be represented by the function $V(y) = 5,000(0.92)^y$, to the nearest cent, which of the following is the value of the car 8 years after its purchase?

    (A) $2,023.68
    (B) $2,566.09
    (C) $3,317.10
    (D) $3,680.00
    (E) $4,149.17

455. If the point $(3, 9)$ lies on the graph of $f(x) = x^3 + x^2 - n$, what is the value of n?

456. If the graph of $f(x) = (x - 4)(x + 1)(x + 6)(x - 9)$ crosses the x-axis at the point $(a, 0)$, then each of the following is a possible value of a EXCEPT

    (A) −6
    (B) −4
    (C) −1
    (D) 4
    (E) 9

457. Given the function $h(x) = \dfrac{x-1}{4}$, if $h(x + 3) = 5$, what is the value of x?

    (A) 14
    (B) 16
    (C) 18
    (D) 21
    (E) 36

458. If the graph of $f(x)$ crosses the x-axis at a single point $(4, 0)$, then at what point will the graph of $f(x) - 6$ cross the x-axis?

    (A) $(-10, 0)$
    (B) $(-6, 0)$
    (C) $(-4, 0)$
    (D) $(-2, 0)$
    (E) This cannot be determined from the information given.

459. If $g(x) = x(x-1)^2$, then at how many values of x does $g(x) = 0$?

(A) None

(B) 1

(C) 2

(D) 3

(E) 4

460. The following figure shows the graph of a function $k(x)$. What is the value of $k\left(\dfrac{8}{3}\right)$?

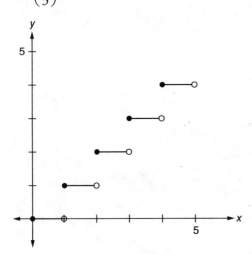

461. A function $f(x)$ is defined such that when $x < 1$, $f(x) = x + 4$, and when $x \geq 1$, $f(x) = 3$. Over which of the following intervals does $f(x)$ reach its maximum value?

(A) $x < -4$

(B) $-4 < x < 0$

(C) $1 < x < 4$

(D) $0 < x < 1$

(E) $x > 4$

462. If $f(a) = \dfrac{a}{2} + 1$, then what is $f(1.2)$?

463. The points $(-2, 0)$ and $(6, 0)$ lie on the graph of a quadratic function $f(x)$. Which of the following could be equivalent to $f(x)$?

(A) $x^2 + 4x - 12$

(B) $x^2 - 2x + 6$

(C) $x^2 + 8x + 12$

(D) $x^2 - 4x - 12$

(E) $x^2 - 2x + 8$

464. If $f(x) = \dfrac{4}{5}x^2$ and $g(x) = \dfrac{1}{2}x + \dfrac{1}{2}$, then which of the following is equivalent to $g(f(x))$?

(A) $\dfrac{2}{5}x^2 + \dfrac{1}{2}$

(B) $\dfrac{4}{7}x^2 + \dfrac{1}{2}$

(C) $\dfrac{4}{9}x^2 + \dfrac{4}{9}$

(D) $\dfrac{1}{5}x^2 + \dfrac{1}{5}x + \dfrac{1}{5}$

(E) $\dfrac{1}{5}x^2 + \dfrac{4}{5}x + \dfrac{1}{5}$

465. Given the following graph of the function $f(x)$, which of the following statements must be true for all values of x?

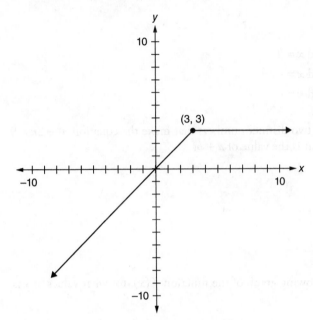

(A) $f(x) < 0$

(B) $f(x) < 1$

(C) $f(x) < 2$

(D) $f(x) < 3$

(E) $f(x) < 4$

466. If the graph of $g(x)$ is a vertical translation of the graph of $f(x) = -x^2 + 1$, then which of the following has the largest value?

(A) $g(-3)$

(B) $g(-2)$

(C) $g(-1)$

(D) $g(0)$

(E) $g(1)$

467. Which of the following represents all of the solutions to the equation
$k(x) = 0$ when $k(x) = x^3(x^2 - 4x + 4)$?

(A) $x = 0$

(B) $x = 2$

(C) $x = 0$ and $x = 2$

(D) $x = 0$ and $x = -2$

(E) $x = 0$ and $x = 4$

468. If a and b are two distinct numbers that make the equation $n^2 - 8n = 9$
true, then what is the value of $a + b$?

(A) -8

(B) -6

(C) 0

(D) 6

(E) 8

469. Given the following graph of the function $f(x)$, for what values of x is
$f(x) > 0$?

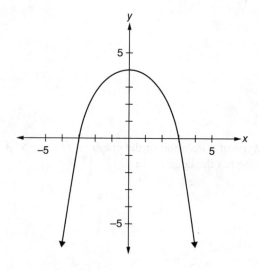

(A) $x < -3$ only

(B) $x > 3$ only

(C) $-3 < x < 3$ only

(D) $0 < x < 4$ only

(E) $x < -3$ and $x > 3$

470. Which of the following statements best describes the graph of a quadratic function $f(x) = ax^2 + bx + c$ where $a > 0$?

(A) The graph has a single minimum value and crosses the x-axis at two distinct points.

(B) The graph has a single minimum value and may or may not cross the x-axis.

(C) The graph has a single maximum value and crosses the x-axis at two distinct points.

(D) The graph has a single maximum value and may or may not cross the x-axis.

(E) The graph may have a single minimum or a single maximum value depending on the sign of b.

471. What is the largest possible number n such that the graphs of $h(x) = x^2 + 3x - 8$ and $k(x) = -4$ intersect at the point (n, y)?

(A) 1

(B) 2

(C) 4

(D) 6

(E) 8

472. If $f(x) = 3x - 1$ and $5f(x) = f(x)$, then $x =$

(A) $\dfrac{1}{5}$

(B) $\dfrac{1}{3}$

(C) 0

(D) 4

(E) 15

473. If for all x, $g(m) = 2m - m^3$, what is the value of $g(-2)$?

(A) -12

(B) -10

(C) -8

(D) 2

(E) 4

474. The graph of a quadratic function $f(x) = ax^2 + bx + c$ reaches a minimum value at a point (x, y). Which of the following inequalities must be true?

(A) $a > 0$

(B) $a < 0$

(C) $a > b$

(D) $a < b$

(E) $a > c$

475. For which of the following possible graphs of a function $f(x)$ is $f(x) > 2$ for all possible values of x?

(A)

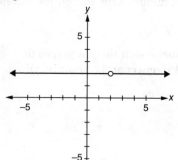

(B)

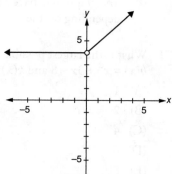

(C)

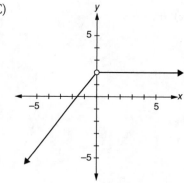

(D)

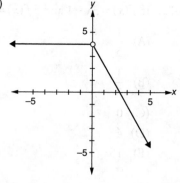

(E)

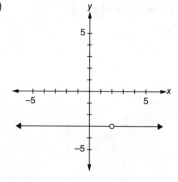

476. If $f(x) = \dfrac{x^2 - x}{2}$, then which of the following is equivalent to $f(2a-1)$?

(A) $2a^2 - 1$

(B) $2a^2 - 3a$

(C) $2a^2 - 6a$

(D) $2a^2 - 2a + 1$

(E) $2a^2 - 3a + 1$

477. If $c > 0$ and $f(x) = 2x - 9$, then which of the following inequalities must be true?

(A) $f(c) > -9$

(B) $f(c) > -\dfrac{9}{2}$

(C) $f(c) > -2$

(D) $f(c) > 0$

(E) $f(c) > 11$

478. If the y-intercept of the graph of a function $f(x)$ is 2, then what is the value of the y-intercept of the graph of $f(x) + 6$?

479. The height, in meters, of a particle after t seconds have passed can be expressed as the function $f(t) = -2t^2 + 32$ for $0 \le t \le 4$. In meters, what is the height of the particle after 2 seconds have passed?

480. For a function $g(x) = x^3 - kx + c$, $g(-1) = 4$ and $g(0) = 10$. What is the value of $k + c$?

(A) -9

(B) -5

(C) 5

(D) 9

(E) 10

481. The following table represents values of a quadratic function $f(x) = ax^2 + bx + c$ for selected values of x. What is the value of the product bc?

x	-3	-2	-1	0
$f(x)$	2	0	0	2

482. If $f(x) = -x^2 + 10x - 21$, then at how many points in the *x-y* plane do the graphs of $f(x)$ and $g(x) = -f(x)$ intersect?

(A) 0

(B) 1

(C) 2

(D) 3

(E) Infinitely many

483. If $f(x) = 5x\sqrt{k}$ and $f(\sqrt{k}) = 35$, then what is the value of *k*?

484. The point $(3, y)$ lies on the graph of the function $h(x) = 4x^2 - x^3$. What is the value of *y*?

(A) 3

(B) 6

(C) 9

(D) 12

(E) 15

485. For a function $f(x) = x^2 - 3$ and a constant *m*, $f(2m+1) = 3m$. Which of the following is the value of $4m^2 + m$?

(A) −4

(B) −3

(C) 0

(D) 2

(E) 4

486. For a number *k*, $g\left(\dfrac{k}{2}\right) = 3k - 2$. Which of the following is equivalent to $g(4k)$?

(A) $3k - 4$

(B) $6k - 2$

(C) $8k - 4$

(D) $12k - 2$

(E) $24k - 2$

487. The following figure shows the graph of the function $f(x)$. What is the value of $f(4) + f(7)$?

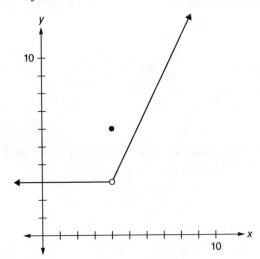

488. The points (0, 5) and (8, 8) lie on the graph of a function $k(x)$. If the points (−5, 5) and (3, 8) lie on the graph of $k(x + m) + n$, then what is the value of $m + n$?

(A) −5

(B) −3

(C) 0

(D) 3

(E) 5

489. Given the functions $f(a) = a - 1$ and $g(a) = a - 2$, for what values of a

does $\dfrac{1}{6} f(a) = \dfrac{1}{g(a)}$?

(A) −1 only

(B) $\dfrac{1}{4}$ only

(C) $\dfrac{7}{6}$ only

(D) 5 and $\dfrac{1}{4}$ only

(E) 4 and −1 only

490. The value of a function f for a given number is found by squaring the difference of that number and 3 and then adding 4. Which of the following is equivalent to $f(x)$?

(A) $x^2 - 5$

(B) $x^2 - 6x + 13$

(C) $x^2 + 13$

(D) $x^2 - 3x + 13$

(E) $x^2 + 1$

491. If the point $\left(x, \dfrac{3}{2}\right)$ lies on the graph of $k(x) = \dfrac{1}{2}(x-1)^2$ and $x > 0$, then $x =$

(A) $\dfrac{1}{8}$

(B) $\dfrac{13}{8}$

(C) $1 + \sqrt{3}$

(D) $\dfrac{\sqrt{6}}{4}$

(E) $\dfrac{\sqrt{6}}{2} + \dfrac{1}{2}$

492. If the point $(-2, 8)$ is on the graph of $f(x) = cx^3$, then $c =$

(A) -1

(B) 0

(C) 1

(D) 2

(E) 3

493. If the graph of a function $f(x)$ never intersects the line $y = 2$, which of the following statements must be true?

   I. There is no value x such that $f(x) = 0$.

   II. There is no value x such that $f(x) = 2$.

   III. The function is undefined at the point $x = 2$.

(A) I only

(B) II only

(C) III only

(D) I and II only

(E) II and III only

494. A function $g(x)$ is defined such that for a function $f(x)$, $g(x) = \dfrac{f(x)}{8}$. If for a constant a, $g(a) = 3$, what is the value of $f(a)$?

495. If $g(x) = \dfrac{|x-1|}{x-1}$ and $x > 1$, which of the following is equivalent to $g(x)$?

(A) -1

(B) 1

(C) $-\dfrac{1}{x-1}$

(D) $\dfrac{1}{x-1}$

(E) This cannot be determined from the information given.

496. A function $f(x)$ is defined for all real values of x. If $f(12) = 11$, then what is the value of $f(13)$?

(A) 11

(B) 12

(C) 13

(D) 14

(E) This cannot be determined from the information given.

497. The graph of $g(x)$ is found by translating the graph of $f(x)$ to the left one unit and up 4 units. Which of the following defines $g(x)$ in terms of $f(x)$?

(A) $f(x+1)+4$

(B) $f(x-1)+4$

(C) $f(x-1)+1$

(D) $f(x+4)-1$

(E) $f(x-4)-1$

498. What is the value of $\dfrac{(f(2))^2}{2}$ if $f(b) = b + b^2$?

499. The graphs of $f(x) = -x^2 + 9$ and $g(x) = x^2 - 9$ intersect at the point (x, y) where x and y are nonnegative. What is the value of $x + y$?

(A) −6

(B) −3

(C) 0

(D) 3

(E) 6

500. The following graph is of the function $g(x) = \dfrac{1}{2} f(x) + 6$ for $x > 0$ and $f(x) = x^2$. What is the value of b?

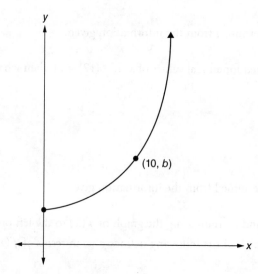

$(10, b)$

ANSWERS

Chapter 1: Numbers

1. (E) Since the remainder when 21 is divided by j is 3, j must divide 18. The factors of 18 less than 9 are 1, 2, 3, and 9, so j must be one of these numbers. The remainder when 30 is divided by 1, 2, 3, and 6 is 0.

2. (D) The formula indicates that the next term of the sequence is found by subtracting the previous term from 1. The first term of the sequence is 2, so the second term must be $1 - 2 = -1$. The third term would then be (1 − the second term) $= 1 - (-1) = 2$.

3. (B) By the given formula, m must be 3 times a multiple of 2. Since we know that m is larger than 45, it is possible to guess and check to find the value of m. Plugging in values for k leads to:

$$3 \cdot 2^1 = 6$$
$$3 \cdot 2^2 = 12$$
$$3 \cdot 2^3 = 24$$
$$3 \cdot 2^4 = 48$$

The first value that is larger than 45 is 48.

4. (D) There are 2 more dollar signs in the chart for 2000 than in 2010. If each dollar sign represents \$25,000, then 2 dollar signs must represent $2 \times \$25,000 = \$50,000$.

5. 6.37. 3.174 rounded to the nearest tenth is 3.2, while rounded to the nearest hundredth it is 3.17. The sum of these values is 6.37.

6. (B) Remember that $a^{-n} = \dfrac{1}{a^n}$. Therefore $m - n = \dfrac{3}{8^2} - \dfrac{5}{8^2} = -\dfrac{2}{8^2} = -\dfrac{2}{64} = -\dfrac{1}{32}$.

7. 54. A prime number is a number larger than 1 that is divisible by only 1 and itself. The largest such number less than 45 is 43, and the largest such number less than 100 is 97.

8. (D) To simplify this expression, try to find any possible perfect cubes (in other words, numbers or expressions that can be written as something to the third power). In this problem, $\sqrt[3]{27x^5} = \sqrt[3]{3^3 x^3 x^2} = 3x\sqrt[3]{x^2}$.

9. (D) Using the formula $a^{-n} = \dfrac{1}{a^n}$, answer choice A is equivalent to -1, while answer choice B is equivalent to 1. Answer choice C is equivalent to $\dfrac{1}{(-1)^2} = 1$. The remaining answer choices are multiples of answer choice C, with D being -2 and E being 2.

10. (D) Since $8^{\frac{j}{k}}$ is a whole number, it must be that $8^{\frac{1}{k}}$ is also a whole number. The only value of k this would be the case for is $k = 3$ (because $8^{\frac{1}{3}} = \sqrt[3]{8} = 2$). Therefore, $8^{\frac{j}{k}} = 8^{\frac{j}{3}} = \left(8^{\frac{1}{3}}\right)^{j} = 2^{j}$. Finally, 16 is 2^4, so $j = 4$ and the product $jk = 12$.

11. $\dfrac{7}{16}$. By counting, we can see the number line is divided into eighths. This means that Q has a value of $\dfrac{5}{8}$, while P is halfway between $\dfrac{1}{8}$ and $\dfrac{2}{8}$. Since half of $\dfrac{1}{8}$ is $\dfrac{1}{16}$, P has a value of $\dfrac{1}{8} + \dfrac{1}{16} = \dfrac{2}{16} + \dfrac{1}{16} = \dfrac{3}{16}$. Finally, $Q - P = \dfrac{5}{8} - \dfrac{3}{16} = \dfrac{10}{16} - \dfrac{3}{16} = \dfrac{7}{16}$.

12. -2. If the first term of the sequence is 4, then the second is $4m$ and the third is $4m^2 = 16$. Solving for m, $m = 2$ or $m = -2$. Since the sixth term is negative, $m = -2$.

13. 160. If $a \nabla 4 = \dfrac{a-4}{4}$ is an integer less than 40, then a must be an integer that is divisible by 4 and, by multiplying both sides of the inequality by 4, $a - 4 < 160$. If $a - 4 < 160$, then $a < 164$, and 164 divided by 4 is 41. Since a must be smaller than 164, check the next multiple of 4, which is $164 - 4 = 160$. $\dfrac{160-4}{4} = \dfrac{156}{4} = 39$.

14. (C) The 7 students that are enrolled in both classes are counted in both counts. Therefore of the history students, only $19 - 7 = 12$ are taking just history, while of the physics students, only $24 - 7 = 17$ are taking just physics, so $12 + 17 = 29$ are taking only one of the courses.

15. (C) In July, the sales at this location were just above \$40,000, so a fair estimate would be about \$41,000, while they were just below \$40,000 in August, or about \$38,000 or \$39,000. Therefore, the total would be closest to \$79,000.

16. (E) $3 \prod (-2) = 2(3) - 4(-2) = 6 + 8 = 14$.

17. 1. Solving the inequality:

$$-3 < 1 - 2x < 3$$
$$-4 < -2x < 2$$
$$2 > x > -1$$

And the smallest positive integer in this range is 1.

18. (A) The problem states that $\sqrt{4a} = 2b^{\frac{1}{2}}$, and squaring both sides of this equation shows that $4a = 4b$, and therefore $a = b$. Since the smallest prime number is 2, b must have a value of 2.

19. (A) If the remainder of x divided by 3, 4, or 11 is zero, then these must be factors of x. Therefore, any factors of these numbers are also factors of x. Since 3 and 4 are factors, then $3 \times 2 = 6$ is also a factor since a factor of 4 is 2.

20. (A) The value of n^2 must be 12 since $n^4 = (n^2)^2 = 144$.

21. (E) The number line is divided into fifths, and so we have $a^{-\frac{1}{2}} = \dfrac{1}{a^{\frac{1}{2}}} = \dfrac{1}{5}$. Squaring both sides of the equation yields $\dfrac{1}{a} = \dfrac{1}{25}$.

22. (D) Equations of the type $|x - a| < b$ are solved using the inequality $-b < x - a < b$, which is equivalent to $a - b < x < a + b$. Working backward, the problem indicates that h should be between 8 and 14, or $8 < h < 14$, which is equivalent to $-3 + 11 < h < 3 + 11$, which is the first step to solving the equation in answer choice (D). In general, this can be found by using the average of the two given numbers inside the absolute value function.

23. (E) Choice I is equivalent since to solve for a you would divide by 14 and $b^2 c^6 = b^2 c^{2 \times 3} = (bc^3)^2$. Since choice II has an incorrect form of this exponent term, it can't be equivalent, while choice III is found by first dividing both sides by 14 and then dividing both sides by b^2 as shown below (recall $\dfrac{1}{b^2} = b^{-2}$).

$$a = \frac{b^2 c^6}{14}$$

$$\frac{a}{b^2} = \frac{c^6}{14}$$

24. (B) Answer choices C, D, and E will all be positive, eliminating them as possible correct answers. Answer choice A will be a value closer to zero than m since n is also a fraction. Finally, answer choice B will be a negative fraction times a positive value larger than 1, leading to a more negative number than that of answer choice A.

25. (B) $5x(\therefore)2 = 3(5x)(2) = 30x = 2y$, and $\partial x = 5x - 1 = 14$. Solving for x in the second equation, $x = 3$ and $30x = 90 = 2y$. Solving this equation for y: $y = 45$. Finally, $3y = 135$.

26. (C) Using the provided equation, $4x - 9 = -19$ or $4x - 9 = 19$. Only the second equation results in x being a positive integer. Solving this equation shows $x = 7$.

27. (C) $\dfrac{m}{n} = \dfrac{\left(\dfrac{p}{q}\right)^4}{\left(\dfrac{q}{p}\right)^{-2}} = \dfrac{\dfrac{p^4}{q^4}}{\dfrac{p^2}{q^2}} = \dfrac{p^2}{q^2} = \left(\dfrac{p}{q}\right)^2.$

28. 84. If x is a multiple of 6 and divisible by 14, it must have the factors 2, 3, and 7. Therefore the smallest value of x is 42. The largest multiple of 42 that is less than 100 is $2 \times 42 = 84$.

29. (A) The numbers in set A are 2, 4, 6, 8, and the numbers in set B are 5, 10, 15. There is no overlap between the sets.

30. (D) $(3x + 1) - (3x - 16) = 17$.

31. (B) For the greatest increase, we must look for the pair of weeks with the biggest height difference between the bars, where the first bar is shorter. This occurs in the second and third weeks.

32. (C) The intersection represents the numbers in both sets. In this case, the intersection consists of the numbers 16, 17, 18, and 19. Of these, only 17 and 19 are prime.

33. 18. Since the -12 is two tick marks from zero, the tick marks must be counting by 6. Since k is three marks above zero, k would be $3 \times 6 = 18$.

34. (C) The given inequality can be written as $n^{\frac{1}{2}} > 5$. Taking both sides to the $\dfrac{1}{m}$ power will result in the inequality $n^{\frac{1}{2m}} > 5^{\frac{1}{m}}$. Since m is a positive integer, $n^{\frac{1}{m}} > n^{\frac{1}{2m}}$. Therefore $n^{\frac{1}{m}} > 5^{\frac{1}{m}}$ or $\sqrt[m]{n} > \sqrt[m]{5}$.

35. (E) The formula tells us that each term in the sequence is half of the term before it. Working backward, if the fifth term is 10, then the fourth term must have been 20, the third term 40, the second term 80, and finally the first term would have to be 160.

36. (C) Plugging in values, only zero will satisfy the inequality since $|0 - 5| = |-5| = 5 < 7$.

37. (A) If j is a multiple of 7 and of $4k$, then j can be written in the form $28k$ or $-28k$ (since a multiple of 7 may be negative). Only answer choice A can be written in this form.

38. (B) In a problem like this, any number in A that is also in B should not be counted in the total. Here, those numbers are 1 and 5. Therefore only the numbers 3, 14, and 21 should be counted.

39. 10.5. 2.144 rounded to the nearest tenth is 2.1, and $2.1 \times 5 = 10.5$.

40. (D) $a^n \cdot a^{-n} \cdot b^{2n} = a^n \cdot \dfrac{1}{a^n} \cdot b^{2n} = \dfrac{a^n}{a^n} \cdot b^{2n} = b^{2n}$.

41. (A) If $(xy)^2 = 36$, then $xy = 6$ or $xy = -6$. So, this problem is essentially asking us to find two numbers whose sum is given and whose product is 6 or -6. Looking at the answer choices,

$-1 = -3 + 2$ and $-3 \times 2 = -6$, while $5 = 2 + 3$ (product is 6) and $7 = 6 + 1$ (product is 6). These answers can be eliminated, leaving A and E. But E could also be written as $12.5 = 12 + 0.5$ and $12 \times 0.5 = 6$, so it can be eliminated. Therefore, the correct answer is A.

42. (E) $|-7 - 1| = |-8| = 8$.

43. 1. All odd integers can be written in the form $2k + 1$, where k is also an integer. Therefore dividing by 2 will leave a remainder of 1.

44. 10. Using the formula, $a_3 = 1 = \dfrac{1}{k}a_2$ and $a_2 = \dfrac{1}{k}(100)$, so $1 = \dfrac{1}{k}\left(\dfrac{1}{k}(100)\right)$. Solving, this equation can be rewritten as $k^2 = 100$, and since k is a positive integer, $k = 10$.

45. (A) $\dfrac{|-3a|}{a} = \dfrac{3|a|}{a}$, which will always have a value of 3 if $a > 0$ and a value of -3 if $a < 0$.

46. (D) $\dfrac{1}{4^{-2}} \cdot \dfrac{3}{2^{-1}} = 4^2 \cdot 3 \cdot 2 = 16 \cdot 6 = 96$.

47. (C) The equation $a[\![\ ]\!](-4) = 3$ is equivalent to $\dfrac{2a}{-4} = 3$. Cross multiplying yields the equation $-12 = 2a$, which has a solution of $a = -6$.

48. (C) The number 21 has two distinct prime factors: 3 and 7. Both of these are less than 10, so the number $21m$ will have also have m as a prime factor.

49. (C) If a is negative, then a^3 will also be negative. Since a negative number divided by a negative number is always positive, selection I will always be positive. For selection II, it is possible a is a number like -11, which would make $a + 10$ negative. But it is also possible that a is a number like -1, which would make $a + 10$ positive. Finally, $2a^{-1} = \dfrac{2}{a}$, which will always be negative since a is negative and 2 is positive.

50. (A) $\left(\dfrac{2}{3}m^3n^{\frac{1}{2}}\right)^2 = \dfrac{2^2}{3^3}m^{3 \cdot 2}n^{\frac{1}{2} \cdot 2} = \dfrac{4}{9}m^6n$.

51. $\dfrac{3}{8}$. Since there are 2 tick marks between every two consecutive whole numbers, the tick marks must represent thirds, and $\dfrac{1}{A} = \dfrac{8}{3}$, which means that A must be the reciprocal, $\dfrac{3}{8}$.

52. $\dfrac{3}{4}$. If $a = 1$, the given equation can be rewritten as $4^3 = 16^{2b}$, and since 16 is 4^2, this equation is equivalent to $4^3 = (4^2)^{2b}$ or $4^3 = 4^{4b}$. Finally, since the bases are the same, $3 = 4b$, which has a solution of $b = \dfrac{3}{4}$.

53. (E) All positive multiples of 5 that are not also multiples of 35 would be in set A but not in set B. Therefore since the multiples of 35 are $35, 70, 105, \ldots$, the numbers that are in set A but not in B include $5, 10, 15, 20, 25, 30, 40, 45, 50, 55, 60, 65, 75, 80, 85, 90,$ $95, 100, 105, \ldots$.

54. (A) Each symbol represents 500 people, and the only difference between January and May is half of one of the symbols. Half of 500 is 250.

55. (D) $(-4)\langle\ \rangle(-1) = \dfrac{1}{2}(-4)^2 - (-1)^2 = \dfrac{1}{2}(16) - 1 = 8 - 1 = 7.$

56. (B) Since a is negative, the square of a will be positive and may be larger than b or c. This eliminates choice I. Additionally, $c + a$ will be a value smaller than c (since a is negative), but it may or may not be larger than b. However, since $c > b$, the difference $c - b > 0$ and therefore must be larger than a.

57. (D) There were 6 teachers who did not attend graduation last year. If the retired teachers were among those that did attend, then there are 2 more teachers (the newly hired teachers) who could attend this year that didn't last year.

58. 4. $-1 \ominus 5 = \dfrac{-(-1 + 5)}{-1} = -1 + 5 = 4.$

59. (A) The expression $\left|-(-x)^2\right|$ is equivalent to $\left|(-x)^2\right| = \left|x^2\right| = x^2$ since the square of any number will be positive. Therefore, x could be 3 or -3.

60. (A) $ab = \dfrac{y}{x}\left(\dfrac{x^2}{y^2}\right) = \dfrac{x}{y}$ since $\dfrac{x}{y} = \dfrac{y}{x} = 1.$

61. (D) If n is a multiple of 11, then any multiple of n will also be a multiple of 11.

62. (C) The distinct prime factors of 6 are 2 and 3, which are both less than 7. Therefore, $6m$ would have $4 + 2 = 6$ distinct prime factors.

63. (B) The equation $|a - b| = |b - a|$ is true for all real values of a and b. The equation $2|a - b| = |b - a|$ therefore implies that 2 times a number is the same as the original number. This only is true when the number is zero. In this case, that is when $|a - b| = 0$, which is only true when $a = b$.

64. (B) Since $m^2 < m$, m must be smaller than 1. Therefore, $\dfrac{n}{m}$ has a denominator that is less than 1. When this occurs, $\dfrac{n}{m} > n.$

65. 5. $270 = 27 \cdot 10 = 3^3 \cdot 2 \cdot 5.$

66. (A) The sum of any two odd integers is even, and any even number is a multiple of 2.

67. (D) The proportion of the circle shaded should be equivalent to the same percentage of the area of the circle. Only answer choice D satisfies this requirement.

68. $\frac{1}{9}$. If, $\left(\frac{x}{3}\right)^2 = 9$ then $\left(\frac{x}{3}\right)^2 = \frac{x^2}{9} = 9$ and $x^2 = 81$. Finally, since x is a positive integer, x must be 9 and $x^{-1} = \frac{1}{9}$.

69. (C) If $\frac{n-1}{5}$ is a positive integer, then $n-1$ must be divisible by 5. The smallest positive integer for which this is true is 5, which means $n = 6$.

70. (B) x will be divisible by any multiple of the given prime numbers, and 8 is not a multiple of 3, 5, or 19.

71. (E) $(a^2)\Phi(4a) = \left(\frac{2a^2}{(4a)^2}\right)^{-3} = \left(\frac{2a^2}{16a^2}\right)^{-3} = \left(\frac{1}{8}\right)^{-3} = 8^3 = 512.$

Chapter 2: Algebra

72. (D) Since 2 is subtracted from x, add 2 to both sides to find the value of x.

73. (C) Let x represent the smallest of the integers. Then $x+1$ will be the larger of the pair, and their sum will be $x + x + 1 = 2x + 1 = 75$. Solving this equation yields $x = 37$.

74. (D) If $4ab = 24$, then $2ab = 12$ and $(2ab)^2 = (12)^2 = 144$.

75. (A) The difference of two numbers is referring to the subtraction of the two numbers, in this case $(a - b)$. This value is the same as "7 less than the sum of the same two numbers." The "sum" always refers to the addition of the two numbers, and here "7 less" implies that we subtract 7 from this value. The whole statement is then $a - b = a + b - 7$.

76. (E) By applying the FOIL method, $(3x - a)(3x + a) = 9x^2 - a^2$. Given that $3x^2 = 2a$, $9x^2 = 3 \cdot 3x^2 = 3 \cdot 2a = 6a$ and $9x^2 - a^2 = 6a - a^2$.

77. (C) Let B stand for Bobby's age, G stand for Gina's age, and A stand for Ann's age. The information given can then be represented as $B = 6 + G$ and $G = 4 + A$. To find out how much older Bobby is than Ann, replace G in the formula $B = 6 + G$ with $G = 4 + A$ to get $B = 10 + A$.

78. (A) The equation $2(m+n) = 8$ is equivalent to $m + n = 4$. Using this value in the equation $2xy = 7(m+n)$ yields $2xy = 28$. Finally, solve for x by dividing both sides by $2y$: $x = \frac{28}{2y} = \frac{14}{y}.$

79. (A) The steps to solving an inequality are the same as the steps for solving an equation. We just must remember that if we divide or multiply both sides by a negative value, the inequality direction switches. In this case, $-3x + 2 < -2x + 4$ is equivalent to $-x + 2 < 4$ which is equivalent to $-x < 2$. The last step is to divide by -1 on both sides, which switches the direction to $x > -2$.

80. (C) Let S represent the cost of the small shirts and L represent the cost of the large shirts. The equation $14L + 10S = 248$ represents the sales on the first day, while the equation $6L + 2S = 88$ represents the sales on the second day. This system of equations has a solution of $L = 12$ and $S = 8$.

81. (E) By factoring out a 2, we can rewrite the equation $2x + 6y = 18$ as $2(x + 3y) = 2(9)$ which implies $x + 3y = 9$.

82. (D) Given both values are positive, $x^2 = 9$ means that $x = 3$, and $xy = 12$ means that $y = 4$. Therefore $(x - 2y)^2 = (3 - 2(4))^2 = (-5)^2 = 25$.

83. (C) Writing the statements as equations: $m = 3n$ and $k = 2n$. Using the first equation, $n = \dfrac{m}{3}$ and therefore $k = 2n = 2\dfrac{m}{3} = \dfrac{2}{3}m$.

84. (D) The total amount of electricity the student used over the n days was $\$nk$. This would leave $\$x - \$nk$ left in the budget.

85. (D) For the first three months, the student paid a total of $3 \times \$15 = \$45$. For the remaining 6 months, the student paid $6 \times \$10 = \$60$. Therefore the student paid a total of $\$45 + \$60 = \$105$.

86. 132. Let the numbers be represented by x and y. The given information then can be written as $x + y = 28$ and $x - y = 16$, which has a solution of $x = 22$ and $y = 6$. The product of 22 and 6 is 132.

87. (A) Since $y = 4$ and $xy = 32$, $x = 8$ and $\dfrac{1}{4}(8) = 2$.

88. 2. Using the FOIL method to simplify the given equation, $a^2 - b^2 = 6$, and since $a^2 = 8$, $8 - b^2 = 6$ and $b^2 = 2$.

89. 23. The sum of 8 and 12 is 20. Three more than this is 23.

90. (B) The given inequality is equivalent to $\dfrac{-5}{2} < x < \dfrac{7}{2}$ or $-2.5 < x < 3.5$. Of the given answer choices, only -2 is between -2.5 and 3.5.

91. (D) Factoring out a 2 in the expression representing a results in the expression $2(x + 2y)$, which is 2 times the expression that represents b.

92. (E) Given the definition $x \oplus y = \dfrac{x+y^2}{x}$, to find $(2xy) \oplus (4xy)$, we must plug in $2xy$ for x and $4xy$ for y:

$$(2xy) \oplus (4xy) = \frac{2xy + (4xy)^2}{2xy} = \frac{2xy + 16x^2 y^2}{2xy} = \frac{2xy(1 + 8xy)}{2xy} = 1 + 8xy.$$

93. (B) We can write the speed of the boat in the form $\dfrac{m \text{ miles}}{1 \text{ hour}} = \dfrac{m \text{ miles}}{60 \text{ min}}$. When determining the distance, multiply by the number of minutes that have elapsed. In this case,

$$n \text{ min} \times \frac{m \text{ miles}}{60 \text{ min}} = \frac{nm}{60} \text{ miles.}$$

94. (E) Start by cross multiplying to rewrite the equation as $\sqrt{x+1} = \dfrac{8}{3}$. Now we square both sides to find $x + 1 = \dfrac{64}{9}$.

95. (C) The given expression can be greatly simplified by factoring:

$$\frac{2x^3 y^4 - x^2 y^2}{x^2 y^2} = \frac{x^2 y^2 (2xy^2 - 1)}{x^2 y^2} = 2xy^2 - 1.$$

Given that xy^2 is 4, $2xy^2 - 1 = 2(4) - 1 = 7$.

96. (D) $9m^2 - 6m + 1 = (3m)^2 - 2(3m) + 1$, which can be factored into $(3m - 1)^2$.

97. (C) Since $pq = r$, we can plug in the other given equation for q to see what it simplifies into. Doing this, we see that $r = pq = p\left(\dfrac{s}{p}\right) = s$.

98. (C) Let P represent the number of pennies in the bag and N represent the number of nickels. The first statement gives us the equation $3N = P$, and the second statement gives us the equation $N + 10 = P - 14$. Solving this system of equations yields $N = 12$ and $P = 36$. Therefore there are $12 + 36 = 48$ pennies and nickels in the bag.

99. 56. Instead of solving the given equation, notice that $\dfrac{7}{4}\sqrt{x} = 7 \times \dfrac{1}{4}\sqrt{x} = 7 \times 8 = 56$.

100. (A) After the raise, the clerk will be paid 12.75 for each hour. This can be written mathematically as $12.75h$.

101. (E) If $\dfrac{2}{3}a \geq 1$, then $a \geq \dfrac{3}{2} = 1.5$. Of the given values, only 2 satisfies this condition.

102. (C) The expression $2x^2 - y - 7$ is equivalent to $2x^2 - y + 1 - 8$, which has a value of $15 - 8 = 7$.

103. 2. If the described integers are represented by x and y, we are told that $x = \dfrac{1}{8}y$. Since x is a fraction of y, we are being asked to determine the smallest possible value of x such that x is an integer larger than 1. If $y = 8$, $x = 1$, so the next largest integer value of y that is divisible by 8 will give us the smallest possible value of x. If $y = 16$, then $x = 2$.

104. (C) If half of Gary's collection was 120 baseball cards, then the full collection must have been $2 \times 120 = 240$ baseball cards.

105. (D) Remember that we must have like denominators before adding two fractions:

$$\frac{x+1}{y} + 8 = \frac{x+1}{y} + \frac{8y}{y} = \frac{x+8y+1}{y}.$$

106. (B) The solution set to $-2 < x + 5 < 9$ is $-7 < x < 4$. Of all these x values, only 1, 2, 3, and 4 are positive integers, and only 3 can be written as $3a$ (let $a = 1$).

107. (E) Solve for x by first subtracting x from both sides to get the equation $x - 7 = 1$ and then adding 7 to both sides to get $x = 8$.

108. (A) The first 3 pounds that were purchased will only last for 2 more months, while the 2 pounds purchased this month will only last for 3 more months.

109. (C) If m and n are two consecutive odd integers such that $m < n$, then $n = m + 2$. Their product would then be $mn = m(m + 2) = m^2 + 2m$.

110. (C) We can represent the value of a with the equation $a = 10 + b$, and we can represent the value of b with the equation $b = c - 7$. Plugging the value of b into the equation for a yields $a = 10 + c - 7 = c + 3$.

111. 11. Multiplying the first equation by -2, we get $-2x + 8y = -30$. Now, by adding equations, we can eliminate the x variable to find $14y = -14$ and $y = -1$. Using the original equation with $y = -1$, we find that $x + 4 = 15$ or $x = 11$.

112. $\dfrac{1}{2}$. If we let x represent the number, then the statement given can be represented as $x^2 = \dfrac{1}{2}x$. This equation can be solved by moving all of the terms to the same side: $x^2 - \dfrac{1}{2}x = 0$ and factoring out an x: $x - \dfrac{1}{2} = 0$. This equation has solutions $x = 0$ and $x = \dfrac{1}{2}$.

113. (D) Using the FOIL method, $\left(\dfrac{1}{5}x - y\right)^2 = \left(\dfrac{1}{5}x - y\right)\left(\dfrac{1}{5}x - y\right) = \dfrac{1}{25}x^2 - \dfrac{2}{5}xy + y^2$.

114. (C) In order to make the recipe 8 times, we will need $8 \times 20\frac{1}{2} = 164$ pounds of flour. Three bags of flour will only provide 150 pounds of flour, so we will need one additional bag.

115. (B) The statement is equivalent to $\sqrt{m+n} = 4m$, and by squaring both sides we get $m+n = (4m)^2 = 16m^2$.

116. (B) If $\frac{a}{b} = 6$, then $\frac{2a}{3b} = \left(\frac{2}{3}\right)\frac{a}{b} = \left(\frac{2}{3}\right)6 = 4$.

117. (A) Since 5 pieces have already been stored and c simply is a count of how many can be stored, there must be room for 5 fewer, or $c - 5$ pieces.

118. (A) If $2xy = 26$ and $0 < x < 4$, then $8y < 26$. In other words, $y < \frac{26}{8} = \frac{13}{4}$. Of the given choices, only 3 is smaller than this value.

119. 4. Remember that dividing by a negative will switch the order of the inequality. With this in mind, if $-9x \leq -28$, then $x \geq \frac{28}{9} = 3.11$. So, the smallest integer possible would be 4.

120. 21. We multiply the equation by $28a$ to get the equivalent equation $7a = 28(3) + 4a$. Subtracting $4a$ from both sides, we see that $4a = 84$ or $a = 21$.

121. (A) The expression $a^2 - 2ab$ is equivalent to $a(a - 2b)$. Therefore answer choice II will never be larger, and answer choice III may or may not be larger depending on the sign of a. Finally choice I is equivalent to $a^2 - 2ab + b^2$. Since the square of any number is always positive, this expression will always be larger.

122. 26. If n is 5 more than 8, $n = 13$. The number m is equal to $2n = 2 \times 13 = 26$.

123. (A) The set contains 10 multiples of 3 that are also multiples of 2. It also contains half this many, or 5, multiples of 5. Therefore, the set contains $40 + 5 = 45$ numbers. The multiples of 3 are already counted in the multiples of 2.

124. (C) Using the given equation, $\frac{1}{2}x = \frac{1}{4}y$, we can find $\frac{3}{4}x$ by multiplying both sides by $\frac{3}{2}$. This yields the equation $\frac{3}{4}x = \frac{3}{8}y$. Finally, adding 1 to each side of the equation yields answer choice C.

125. (D) If $2 \ominus n = 9$, then $3(2)^2 - n = 9$ or $n = 3$.

126. (B) $\frac{x}{2} - y$ is equivalent to $\frac{1}{2}(x - 2y)$. Since $x - 2y = 8$, $\frac{x}{2} - y = \frac{1}{2}(8) = 4$.

127. (E) We would have to add 8 to the expression $6a - 3$ to get the expression $6a + 5$.

128. (C) The given inequality simplifies to $1 < m < 4.5$. Therefore if x is a solution, x is between 1 and 4.5. In this case, half of x may be a solution since if $x = 4$, half of x is 2 and both numbers are in the given range. Further, $2x$ may be a solution since if $x = 2$, $2x = 4$ and both are again within the range. However, even if x is the smallest possible value in the range, $5x$ will be larger than 4.5.

129. (C) The phrase "6 more than" implies we should add 6 to the number of red marbles to get the number of green marbles, or $r + 6$. Then the total number of marbles in the urn would be the number of red marbles plus the number of green marbles, or $r + r + 6 = 2r + 6$.

130. $\dfrac{4}{3}$. We start by subtracting x from both sides of the equation to get $-2 = 3x - 6$. Next, we add 6 to both sides and find $4 = 3x$. Finally, dividing both sides by 3 will yield the value of x.

131. (B) Since $p = 2q$, $4p + q = k = 4(2q) + q = 8q + q = 9q$.

132. (E) $\dfrac{1}{2}\left(\dfrac{3x}{y} + \dfrac{1}{6}\right) = \dfrac{1}{2}\left(\dfrac{18x}{6y} + \dfrac{y}{6y}\right) = \dfrac{1}{2}\left(\dfrac{18x + y}{6y}\right) = \dfrac{18x + y}{12y}$.

133. (E) $\dfrac{5 \text{ mi}}{36 \text{ min}}(45 \text{ min}) = \dfrac{5}{4}(5) \text{ mi} = \dfrac{25}{4} \text{ mi}$.

134. 14. Two times $2ab - a$ is $4ab - 2a$. This is equal to 10 since $2ab - a = 5$. Adding 4 to this value results in a total of 14.

135. (B) The given inequalities can be simplified to $x < \dfrac{11}{6} \approx 1.8$ and $-3 < x < 3$. The only positive integer that satisfies both inequalities is 1.

136. (C) Using FOIL, we can rewrite the given inequality as $m^2 + 2mn + n^2 \le m^2 - 2mn + n^2$ or $2mn \le -2mn$. Now, dividing by -2 on both sides and remembering that the direction of the inequality will switch, we see that $-mn \ge mn$. This statement will only be true if mn is negative. Since mn is a product, that will only occur if m and n have opposite signs.

137. $\dfrac{17}{16}$. We start by squaring both sides of the equation to get $x - 1 = \dfrac{1}{16}$. The value of x is now found by adding 1 to both sides of this equation.

138. (A) In terms of a, $b = \dfrac{1}{4}a$. Therefore, if $a > 14$, $b > \dfrac{1}{4}(14) = \dfrac{7}{2}$.

139. (E) Adding the two equations will result in the equation $m + 3n = 18$.

140. (D) The information given can be written as the equation $\frac{2}{3}x = 5y$. Therefore, $15y = 3\left(\frac{2}{3}x\right) = 2x$.

141. (C) For each performance, the magician must use x envelopes. For example, for 3 performances she would need $x + x + x = 3x$ envelopes. Therefore for y performances, she would need xy envelopes.

142. (A) Factoring ab out of the expression will reduce each exponent by 1: $ab^3 - ab^4 + a^2b^2 = ab(b^2 - b^3 + ab)$.

Chapter 3: Probability, Statistics, and Sequences

143. (A) $\frac{5x + 3x + 2x + 8x}{4} = \frac{18x}{4} = \frac{9x}{2}$.

144. (A) When two events are independent, we multiply their probabilities to find the probability both will occur. Here, $0.25 \times 0.30 = 0.075$.

145. (B) The set contains the integers 2, 3, 4, 5, 6, 7, 8, 9, 10, 11, 12, 13, and 14. Only 3 of these 13 numbers are smaller than 5, so the probability is $\frac{3}{13}$.

146. 20. $\frac{3}{4}(80) = 60$ people are older than 25, so $80 - 60 = 20$ people must be 25 or younger.

147. (C) The median is the middle value when the numbers are placed in order. In this case, that is 4.

148. (D) Let x represent the sum of the 8 numbers. Then since the mean is 4, $\frac{x}{8} = 4$ or $x = 32$.

149. (D) Let B represent the number of blue coins. Then, since there are twice as many red coins as blue, the total number of coins in the jar is $2B + B = 3B$. Therefore the probability of selecting a blue coin is $\frac{B}{3B} = \frac{1}{3}$.

150. (E) There are 5 odd numbers in the given range. By the multiplication rule of counting, we can find the total number of passwords with the product $5 \times 5 \times 5 \times 5 = 625$.

151. (D) The area of the larger circle is found using the area formula for a circle: πr^2. Thus, it must be that the area of the smaller circle is $\frac{1}{2}\pi r^2$ and the average area of the two is $\dfrac{\frac{1}{2}\pi r^2 + \pi r^2}{2} = \dfrac{\frac{3}{2}\pi r^2}{2} = \frac{3}{4}\pi r^2$.

152. (C) Since the list is made up of consecutive integers and the median, or middle number, is 3, the list must be 1, 2, 3, 4, 5. Therefore when 5 is added to each term, the list is 6, 7, 8, 9, 10. The median of this list is 8.

153. (E) The order of the books selected does not matter. This means this is a combination problem and the number of different ways to select the books is $15 \times 14 \times 13 \times 12 = 32{,}760$.

154. (D) If the average of p, q, and r is 12, then $\dfrac{p+q+r}{3} = 12$ and $p+q+r = 36$. Including the information about m, we see that $\dfrac{p+q+r+m}{4} = 20$ and $p+q+r+m = 80$. Since we know $p+q+r = 36$, it must be that $m = 80 - 36 = 44$.

155. (A) The nth term of any geometric sequence can be found with the formula $a_n = a_1 r^{n-1}$, where r is the ratio used to find the next term. Using the given information, $a_{30} = k = a_1 \left(\dfrac{1}{2}\right)^{29}$. Solving for a_1, we see that $a_1 = \dfrac{k}{\left(\dfrac{1}{2}\right)^{29}} = \dfrac{k}{\dfrac{1}{2^{29}}} = 2^{29} \times k$.

156. (B) Let the total number of students in the class be represented by x. Since the probability of selecting a senior is $\dfrac{5}{9}$ and there are 15 seniors, we can write $\dfrac{15}{x} = \dfrac{5}{9}$, which simplifies to $135 = 5x$ or $x = 27$. If there are 27 students in the class and 15 are seniors, then $27 - 15 = 12$ must be juniors.

157. (E) The first 10 terms of the sequence are a, b, c, a, b, c, a, b, c, a, while the next 10 terms are b, c, a, b, c, a, b, c, a, b. With this continuing pattern, the next 10 terms will end in the letter c. So the 10th term of the sequence is a, the 20th is b, and the 30th is c. This pattern will continue, so the 50th term will be b while the 90th term will be c.

158. 6. If the number created is always less than 2,000, the first digit must be 1. There are then 3 ways to pick the second digit, 2 ways to pick the third digit, and 1 way to pick the fourth digit. By the multiplication principle, this means there are $1 \times 3 \times 2 \times 1 = 6$ ways to arrange the numbers.

159. (A) $\dfrac{(2x)+(x+4)+5}{3} = \dfrac{3x+9}{3} = x+3$.

160. 17. Since there are an even number of numbers in the list, the median will be the average of the two middle numbers. In this case, that is the average of the fifth and sixth numbers in the list. Therefore if the sixth integer is x, $\dfrac{11+x}{2} = 14$ or $11 + x = 28$. This equation has a solution of $x = 17$.

161. 72. If there are 4 choices for an appetizer, there must be 2 choices for an entrée and 9 choices for a dessert. By the multiplication principle, there are $4 \times 2 \times 9 = 72$ choices for the special.

162. **(D)** The given information can be written as $\dfrac{S_1}{10} = x$ and $\dfrac{S_2}{10} = y$, where S_1 and S_2 are the sums of the two sets of numbers, respectively. The sum of all 20 numbers is therefore $S_1 + S_2 = 10x + 10y = 10(x + y)$.

163. **(D)** There are 11 people in front of Jackie and 11 people behind Jackie. Therefore there are 22 people in line besides Jackie, or 23 people total in line when Jackie is included.

164. 4. The median is the middle value when the numbers are listed in order. If we were to write out a list of the number of plays each patron has seen, there would be 92 numbers in the list. The median therefore would be the average of the 46th and the 47th numbers in the list. The first 25 numbers would be 2s, while the next 15 numbers would be 3s. This brings us to the 40th number on the list, and from here until the 75th number on the list, the values are all 4. Therefore, the 46th and 47th numbers on the list are 4s and the median is 4.

165. 150. Let the first integer be represented by x. Since the average of the three is 150, $\dfrac{x + x + 1 + x + 2}{3} = \dfrac{3x + 3}{3} = x + 1 = 150$. This means the three integers are 149, 150, and 151. The median of this list is 150.

166. **(A)** Since the median is 9, it must be that x is larger than 9 (or otherwise the median would be shifted). Therefore, the median cannot be 5.

167. **(C)** The probability of a simple event is the number of ways that event can happen out of the total. When selecting a coin, there are 8 ways to select a quarter and 64 ways to select a coin in general. Therefore the probability of selecting a quarter is $\dfrac{8}{64} = \dfrac{1}{8}$.

168. **(A)** The median of this data set will be the middle number, or the 90th number if the ages are written in a list from smallest to largest. Since the first 150 numbers would be smaller than 38, the median would also be smaller than 38.

169. **(B)** The first digit can be any number 1 through 9, while the second digit can only be 3, 6, or 9. Therefore there are $9 \times 3 = 27$ possible numbers of this form.

170. $\dfrac{1}{2}$. To earn 2 points, an odd number must have been selected. There are 5 out of 10 numbers that are odd, so the probability of selecting such a number is $\dfrac{5}{10} = \dfrac{1}{2}$.

171. **(C)** Following the pattern, the terms of the sequence can be easily written out. They are 104, 52, 48, 24, 20, 10, 6, 3, −1, . . . As we can see, the ninth term is the first term smaller than 1.

172. **(B)** Joseph spends a total of 10 hours a day at school, and 3 of those hours are not in classes. Therefore the probability is $\dfrac{3}{10}$.

173. (D) If there are 3 symbols and the first one is chosen randomly, then there is a 1 in 3 chance γ will be first.

174. (C) Let H represent Hilda's age and F represent Frank's age. Using the given information, $H = F + 3$ and $F = G - 6$. Plugging the second equation into the first, $H = G - 6 + 3 = G - 3$. The average of their ages would then be $\dfrac{H + F + G}{3} = \dfrac{G - 3 + G - 6 + G}{3} = \dfrac{3G - 9}{3} = G - 3$.

175. (D) $0.75(82) + 0.25(79) = 81.25$.

176. 1. If the median is 15, it simply means the middle value of the ordered list is 15. The first value could be any positive integer from 1 to 15. For example, the list 1, 14, 15, 100, 1,000 has a median of 15.

177. (E) The described sequence is arithmetic, and the formula for the nth term of any arithmetic sequence is $a_n = a_1 + (n-1)d$, where d is the term being added to find subsequent terms. For the 19th term of this sequence, $a_{19} = x + (19 - 1)n$.

178. (D) There are 3 possible paths from A to B, and from here any one of 4 paths can be taken to C. Therefore there are 3×4 total possible paths.

179. (C) There are 9 ways to pick the first officer, 8 ways to pick the next, and 7 ways to pick the next. By the multiplication principle, there are $9 \times 8 \times 7$ ways to pick all three officers.

180. $\dfrac{89}{90}$. There are a total of 89 two-digit numbers that are less than 99 (all the whole numbers from 10 to 98 (found by subtracting the number of one-digit numbers from 98, or $98 - 9 = 89$) and a total of 90 two-digit numbers altogether (including 99), so the probability is $\dfrac{89}{90}$.

181. (C) $\dfrac{2x^2 + 4x}{2} = x^2 + 2x$.

182. (B) If the base of the smaller triangle is represented by b and the height of the smaller triangle is represented by h, the areas of the two triangles would be $\dfrac{1}{2}bh$ and $\dfrac{1}{2}b(3h)$. The average would then be $\dfrac{\dfrac{1}{2}bh + \dfrac{3}{2}bh}{2} = \dfrac{\dfrac{4}{2}bh}{2} = \dfrac{2bh}{2} = bh = 10$. The area of the smaller triangle is $\dfrac{1}{2}bh$, so it is $\dfrac{10}{2} = 5$.

183. (B) Since we are given the third and fifth terms, we can say that $108r^2 = 3{,}888$, since multiplying by r once would give the fourth term and multiplying by r again would give the fifth term. This equation simplifies to $r^2 = 36$, which has a positive solution of 6.

184. (C) If 2 is subtracted from each number in the set, the result is 2, 4, 5, 12, 16, and 19. Only 3 out of the 6 numbers would have a remainder of zero when divided by 4. Therefore the probability this process will result in a remainder of zero is $\frac{3}{6} = \frac{1}{2}$.

185. (D) If one more box brought the total of blue paper to 5, there must have originally been 4 blue boxes and 4 orange boxes. There are now 4 orange boxes of 9 total boxes.

186. (A) Because one of each type is picked, the multiplication rule applies, leading to a total of mnp choices.

187. (A) The previous term is represented by a_{n-1}, and in order, 5 times this is $5a_{n-1}$ and 2 fewer is $5a_{n-1} - 2$.

188. 20. Looking at each digit, the first digit must be 1 and the second must be 0 for the resulting number to be less than 1,100. The third digit can be any number from 0 to 9, and the last digit must be either 5 or 7. Therefore there are $1 \times 1 \times 10 \times 2 = 20$ possible numbers with these properties by the multiplication rule.

189. (C) The order of the two selected does not matter; therefore this is a combination and $_{20}C_2 = 20 \times 19 = 380$.

190. (A) If the median is $-2x$, then its value must be between the values of x and x^2. This is only true for answer choice A.

191. $\frac{1}{6}$. There is one outcome of six that would result in a 3 coming up on a single roll.

192. 120. By the multiplication rule $5 \times 4 \times 3 \times 2 = 120$.

193. (D) If x is a fraction, each power of x will be smaller than the previous. In order from least to largest, this data set is written as x^4, x^3, x^2, x, and $3x$, and the median is x^2.

194. (A) The line through the center accounts for a central angle of 180 degrees, and 150 of that is in segment A. Therefore segment B accounts for $\frac{30}{360}$ central degrees in the circle, or $\frac{1}{12}$ of the area.

195. (D) For a list of 6 numbers, the median will be the average of the two middle numbers. Since the median is 85 minutes, $\frac{\text{third time} + \text{fourth time}}{2} = 85$ and third time + fourth time $= 170$.

196. (D) The median is just the middle number, which in this case would be n, and the mean would be $\frac{10n}{10} = n$.

197. (E) There are a total of 6 symbols. Since the symbols can be selected twice, there are $6 \times 6 = 36$ ways to select two of the symbols.

198. (C) Since the numbers are unique, removing the 5 largest numbers will cause the mean to be smaller.

199. (D) Given that the mean of the x's is 3, we can write $\dfrac{x_1 + x_2 + x_3 + x_4}{4} = 3$, so $x_1 + x_2 + x_3 + x_4 = 12$. Further, $\dfrac{x_1 + x_2 + x_3 + x_4 + y_1 + y_2 + y_3}{7} = 6$, so $x_1 + x_2 + x_3 + x_4 + y_1 + y_2 + y_3 = 42$. Given the first sum we found, $y_1 + y_2 + y_3 = 42 - 12 = 30$, therefore $\dfrac{y_1 + y_2 + y_3}{3} = 10$.

200. (C) If the two events cannot occur at the same time, the probability of one or the other occurring is the sum of their individual probabilities. Here, $\dfrac{x}{4} + \dfrac{3x}{8} = \dfrac{2x}{8} + \dfrac{3x}{8} = \dfrac{5x}{8}$.

201. $\dfrac{64}{3}$. Plugging 8 into the given expressions and ordering from least to greatest yields $\dfrac{16}{3}, \dfrac{56}{3}, 24, 80$. Since there are an even number of values in the list, the median is the average of the two middle values or $\dfrac{\dfrac{56}{3} + 24}{2} = \dfrac{56}{6} + 12 = \dfrac{56 + 72}{6} = \dfrac{128}{6} = \dfrac{64}{3}$.

202. (B) The number 1 will be the middle value of the list. However, the number 3 will be part of the calculation for the mean, making it larger than 1.

203. (E) Based on the given information, if we were to write a list of the number of new movies Joe has seen in the past 5 years it would look like 10, _____, 14, _____, 20. Therefore the smallest the mean could be is if the 10 and the 14 were repeated: $\dfrac{10 + 10 + 14 + 14 + 20}{5} = 13.6$. Only answer E is larger than this value.

204. 122. If the value of x is 1 (the smallest positive integer) and y is 122, then the probability of picking one of these numbers is $\dfrac{1}{122}$.

205. 2. The pattern repeats every 7 numbers. For example, the 7th, 14th, 21st, 49th, and 70th numbers in the sequence have a value of 4 because they are multiples of 7. Continuing this pattern, since $98 = 7 \times 14$, the 98th digit is 4, meaning the 99th is 1 and the 100th is 2.

206. (C) In a list of 8 numbers, the median will be the average of the fourth and fifth numbers. The fourth number will be $15 + (3 \times 10) = 45$, and the fifth number will be $15 + (4 \times 10) = 55$. In this case, $med = \dfrac{45 + 55}{2} = \dfrac{100}{2} = 50$.

207. $\dfrac{1}{10}$. Any three-digit number less than 150 with a ones digit of 7 must have a 1 as the first digit, any value from 0 to 4 as the second digit, and a 7 as the third digit. There are $1 \times 5 \times 1 = 5$ such numbers. Further, there are 50 three-digit numbers less than 150 (this includes 100), so the probability such a number is generated is $\dfrac{5}{50} = \dfrac{1}{10}$.

208. (C) If $\dfrac{3x + 5x + 2x - 1 + x + 1}{4} = 8$, then $11x = 32$ and $x = \dfrac{32}{11}$. Therefore, the mean of x and $x + 2$ is $\dfrac{\dfrac{32}{11} + \dfrac{32}{11} + 2}{2} = \dfrac{64}{22} + 1 = \dfrac{86}{22} = \dfrac{43}{11}$.

209. (D) Selecting a red or blue marble is the complementary event to selecting a green marble. Therefore the probability of it occurring is $1 - \dfrac{2}{9} = \dfrac{9}{9} - \dfrac{2}{9} = \dfrac{7}{9}$.

210. (B) There are a total of 15 students, of which 2 are sophomores.

211. (B) $\dfrac{\sqrt{2} + 5\sqrt{2}}{2} = \dfrac{6\sqrt{2}}{2} = 3\sqrt{2}$.

212. $\dfrac{7}{4}$. In a list with an even number of values, the median is the average of the two middle numbers. Since the two middle numbers in this case are the same, their average must have the same value as the numbers (e.g., the average of 5 and 5 is 5).

213. 12. Denote the smallest integer as x. Then, $\dfrac{x + (x+1) + (x+2) + (x+3) + (x+4) + (x+5)}{6} = \dfrac{6x + 15}{6} = \dfrac{29}{2}$. Multiplying by 6, this equation is equivalent to $6x + 15 = 87$. Solving this equation yields $x = 12$.

Chapter 4: Coordinate Geometry

214. (A) The origin refers to the point $(0, 0)$. Using the formula for slope, $m = \dfrac{0 - 5}{0 - (-1)} = -5$.

215. (D) If a point is on the line, plugging the values for x and y into the equation of the line will yield a true statement. For answer choice D, $y = 2 = 3(1) - 1$.

216. (D) Any line perpendicular to the given line will have a slope of $\dfrac{3}{2}$, the negative reciprocal of the slope of the original line, $-\dfrac{2}{3}$. Additionally, the given point has an x-value of 0, meaning it is the y-intercept of the line we want to find. Using point intercept form, the equation of the line must be $y = \dfrac{3}{2}x + \dfrac{1}{8}$.

217. (C) A completely horizontal line will have a slope of 0. In this case, the line closest to this is line C.

218. (D) The length of line segment $\overline{PQ}$ is 5 units (from -1 to 4). Moving 5 units from the right of -3 (from point M) would yield an x-value of 2.

219. (E) A line with the form $y = mx$ will pass through the origin. Therefore, the slope is
$$m = \frac{8-0}{2-0} = 4.$$

220. (C) Line segments $\overline{PR}$ and $\overline{RQ}$ must have a length of 3. Also, since $\overline{PQ}$ is the same length as $\overline{RS}$, $\overline{QS}$ also has a length of 3. $PS = PQ + QS = 6 + 3 = 9$.

221. (A) For a line to be parallel to the given line, it must only have the same slope.

222. (B) The equation is of the form $y = mx + b$, where b is the y-intercept.

223. (D) For a linear equation, the change in y must be the same for a corresponding change in x. Here, each x value is increased by 1 and the two given y values have a difference of 4. Therefore, there must be a change of 2 for each 1 unit increase in x.

224. (B) Line PQ has a slope of $\dfrac{5}{4}$ since there is an increase of 5 units in y for an increase in 4 units of x. $\overline{MN}$ would have the same slope since M is 5 units down and N is 4 units to the right of the origin.

225. (B) Since the second tick mark is 6, the first tick mark must be 3. Counting by 3s until we reach the point yields the y value of 15.

226. (B) Since the lines are parallel and the slope of ℓ is undefined, then both lines are vertical. As both lines are vertical, line m would pass through (2, 4) and the distance between this point and (0, 4), the point known on ℓ, would be 2.

227. (E) If Chuck's house is the point (0, 0) on the coordinate plane, then Carly's house would be (2, 5). The straight-line distance is then $d = \sqrt{(2-0)^2 + (5-0)^2} = \sqrt{4+25} = \sqrt{29}$.

228. (B) We are given the slope and the y-intercept, so we can write the equation of the line: $y = -3x + 6$. The question asks us to find the x-intercept, which is found by solving $0 = -3x + 6$. So $3x = 6$ and $x = 2$.

229. (B) The described graph should show a steady increase followed by a break and then a steady increase that is a little less steep.

230. (B) Any equation of the form $y = c$ is a horizontal line and will have a slope of zero.

231. (A) Line ℓ must have a slope that is the negative reciprocal of the slope of $3y + x = 4$. The slope of $3y + x = 4$ can be found by writing that equation in slope intercept form, or by solving for y. This form is $y = \dfrac{4}{3} - \dfrac{1}{3}x$, and so the slope of ℓ must be 3 (the negative reciprocal of $-\dfrac{1}{3}$). Since we are given the y-intercept of ℓ, we can say the equation of ℓ is $y = 3x - 5$. On this line, when $x = -4$, $y = -17$.

232. 50. The total angle must be 180, and the total of the 3 x's must be $180 - 30 = 150$. If $3x = 150$, then $x = 50$.

233. **(C)** $m = \dfrac{(t+9)-(t+4)}{(t+7)-t} = \dfrac{5}{7}$.

234. **(C)** The given angles must have a sum of 180. The equation $(4x - 3) + (2x - 3) = 180$ has a solution of 31.

235. **(A)** A line that is perpendicular to another line will always have the negative reciprocal slope of the other line. Therefore, the product of the two slopes will always be -1.

236. **(D)** The length of the hypotenuse will be the distance from $(0, 1)$ to $(1, 4)$, or $\sqrt{(1-0)^2 + (4-1)^2} = \sqrt{1+9} = \sqrt{10}$.

237. $\dfrac{7}{16}$. Two parallel lines will have the same slope. If we let this common slope be x then $2x = \dfrac{7}{8}$ and $x = \dfrac{7}{16}$.

238. **(D)** The distance from the midpoint to one endpoint is half the total length of the line.

239. **(B)** Since the lines are perpendicular, the angle between them must be 90 degrees and $2x + y = 90$. Since $2x = y$, this equation is equivalent to $2y = 90$ or $y = 45$.

240. **(D)** Using the points $P(-4, 0)$ and $Q(-1, 1)$ in the point-slope form of a line, the equation should be $y - 0 = \dfrac{1-0}{-1-(-4)}(x - (-4))$, which simplifies to $y = \dfrac{1}{3}x + \dfrac{4}{3}$.

241. **(B)** If the lines are parallel, they have the same slope. Therefore if that slope is k, then their product $k^2 = c$ and $k = \sqrt{c}$.

242. **(C)** Reflection of a point (x, y) across the line $y = x$ results in the point (y, x).

243. **(B)** Since m and n are parallel, $p = w$ and $q = z$. Therefore, since $p = 2q$, it must be that $w = 2z$. Solving for z in this equation results in $\dfrac{w}{2} = z$.

244. (A) A line with a positive slope will rise from left to right. If the line passes through the origin and A, this will be the case.

245. (E) The point $(1, 4)$ is 1 unit away from the x-axis and 4 units away from the y-axis.

246. 240. The angle directly across from 60 must also have a measure of 60 degrees. Since these lines intersect, the total of all the angles must be 360. Therefore $x + y = 360 - 120 = 240$.

247. 2. Since the figures are rectangles, $\overline{MN}$ and $\overline{ST}$ are straight line segments. Further, since the point M has an x-coordinate of 1, the point N has coordinates $(1, 0)$. Similarly, using point S, point T has coordinates $(3, 0)$. The distance between these points is 2.

248. (B) If the line has a slope of 1, it must be of the form $y = x + b$. Plugging in the values from the given point, $5 = 1 + b$ and $b = 4$. Therefore, the equation of the line is $y = x + 4$, and any point on the line will have the form $(x, x + 4)$. Every point except choice B has this form.

249. (E) Any line parallel to the x-axis will have the form $y = c$ for some constant c. Since the y-coordinate of the given point is 2, the line m is $y = 2$ and crosses the y-axis at the point $(0, 2)$.

250. (D) If we let P be the point $(0, 0)$ in the x-y plane, then T would have the coordinates $(4, 4)$ and the distance would be $\sqrt{(4-0)^2 + (4-0)^2} = \sqrt{32} = 4\sqrt{2}$.

251. 18. since B is the midpoint of $\overline{AC}$, it must be that $\overline{AB}$ has a length of 4 (the length of $\overline{BC}$). Therefore the length of $\overline{AD}$ is $4 + 4 + 10 = 18$.

252. (D) If $m + n = 0$, then $m = -n$. Two lines are parallel when they have the same slope, so since $-m = n$, the line with slope $-m$ must be parallel to the line with slope n.

253. (A) Since Q is on the x-axis, $y = 0$, and since the line segment has a length of 6, $x = 7$. Therefore, $y - x = 0 - 7 = -7$.

254. (C) Solving for y will result in a line in slope-intercept form. In this form, the coefficient of x is the slope of the line. In this case, $x - 10 = -5y$ and $-\dfrac{1}{5}x + 2 = y$.

255. (E) The slope of line AB is $\dfrac{4-0}{0-(-3)} = \dfrac{4}{3}$, so the slope of BC must be $\dfrac{1}{2}\left(\dfrac{4}{3}\right) = \dfrac{4}{6} = \dfrac{2}{3}$. On line BC, for every 3-unit increase in x, we will see an increase of 2 units in y. From B to C there is an increase of 3 units in x, therefore y must be $4 + 2 = 6$.

256. (B) From -1 to 1, there is a 2-unit increase, and from 6 to 2, there is a 4-unit decrease. Since f is linear, this pattern will continue and a must be $2 - 4 = -2$.

257. (B) The total $x + 2y$ must be 180 degrees since AB is a straight line. Therefore, $x = 180 - 2y$.

258. (D) Any equation that passes through the origin will have the form $y = mx$ when it is in slope-intercept form or $ay + bx = 0$ when it is in standard form (m, a, and b are real numbers).

259. (C) When a point (x, y) is reflected across the x-axis, the resulting point is $(x, -y)$.

260. (B) The slope of line QR would be $\dfrac{5-0}{0-5} = \dfrac{5}{-5} = -1$.

261. (B) In 12 hours, there will be a total of 3 hour-long breaks where no miles are driven resulting in a flat line. Additionally, each driving period of 3 hours is at a constant speed, so the lines representing the time spent driving will show a steady increase in miles covered.

262. (C) Since m and n are perpendicular, the angle between the lines must be 90 degrees. Therefore, $25 + x = 90$ or $x = 90 - 25 = 65$.

263. (A) Any line with an undefined slope will have the form $x = c$ for some constant c. Since the x-coordinate of the given point is -7, each point on the line must also have an x-coordinate of -7 and the equation of the line is $x = -7$.

264. (E) The radius of the described circle is the distance between the two given points: $\sqrt{(4-1)^2 + (6-3)^2} = \sqrt{18} = 3\sqrt{2}$. Therefore, the area is $\pi r^2 = \pi\left(3\sqrt{2}\right)^2 = 18\pi$.

265. (C) The third tick mark on both the x and y axes is 12. Thus each tick mark must represent 4, and the point Q is $(-4, 20)$. So $x + y = -4 + 20 = 16$.

266. (B) $m = \dfrac{2y - y}{2x - x} = \dfrac{y}{x}$.

267. (C) Any point on the x-axis will have the form $(x, 0)$, and any point on the y-axis will have the form $(0, y)$. For this reason, the product of the x-coordinates will always be 0.

268. (B) The angle between the two intersecting lines is 90 degrees, so $2y = 90$ and $3x = 90$. This means that $y = 45$, $x = 30$, and $x + y = 75$.

269. (E) For every hour, the plane travels 200 miles. Therefore to get to point N, the plane travels north 200 miles, west 600 miles, and north again for 400 miles. The total distance north is 600 miles, and this will be the y-coordinate of N. The direction west would be in the negative direction of x, and this total distance is 600 miles, or a coordinate of -600.

270. (E) The slope of a line is defined as the change in y "over" the change in x. In this case, $\dfrac{d-b}{c-a} = \dfrac{-15}{-5} = 3$.

271. (A) Since m and n are parallel lines and the two angles are alternate interior angles, $x + 55 = 110$. Solving this equation for x, $x = 55$.

272. (E) As shown in the figure, since D is the midpoint of line segment $\overline{CE}$ and $\overline{CD}$ has a length of 3, $\overline{DE}$ must also have a length of 3. Although the length of $\overline{BC}$ is unknown, it is known that it must be positive. Therefore, the total length must be larger than 9.

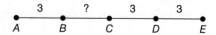

273. (A) The definition of slope comes from the concept of "rise over run" $\left(\dfrac{\text{rise}}{\text{run}}\right)$ or the change in y divided by the change in x. To get from point P to point Q, we must move down two units (-2 for rise) and to the left 3 units (-3 for run), giving a slope of $m = \dfrac{-2}{-3} = \dfrac{2}{3}$. If this is m, then $\dfrac{m}{2} = \dfrac{1}{3}$. The best two possible answer choices are $\overline{PR}$ and $\overline{PT}$, but closer inspection reveals that to get from P to T, we would go up one unit and then to the left 3, giving us a slope of $-\dfrac{1}{3}$, while going from P to R we would move down one and to the left 3, giving a slope of $\dfrac{-1}{-3} = \dfrac{1}{3}$.

274. 5.099. The smallest possible value of k is 1. If k is 1, then the coordinates of A are $(1, 1)$ and the coordinates of B are $(6, 2)$. Using the distance formula, the minimum possible distance is $\sqrt{(2-1)^2 + (6-1)^2} = \sqrt{26} \approx 5.099$.

275. (B) Let the angle between q and r be represented by x. Given this, along line P, the total angle measure should be 180 degrees. Since the angle between p and r is 80 and the angle between p and q is 35, we can write that $80 + 35 + x = 180$ or $115 + x = 180$. Solving for x, $x = 180 - 115 = 65$.

276. (D) The x-coodinate does not change along line segment $\overline{MN}$, so the length of this line segment is $3 + 5 = 8$. Using the fact that $\overline{MN}$ and $\overline{NP}$ are perpendicular, it must be that the y-coordinates do not change along $\overline{NP}$. Further, the length of $\overline{NP}$ is half the length of $\overline{MN}$, so the length is 4 and the coordinates for P are $(2 + 4, 3)$ or $(6, 3)$. Finally, using the distance formula, the distance between M and P is $\sqrt{(6-2)^2 + (3+5)^2} = \sqrt{80} = 4\sqrt{5}$.

277. (D) Since lines m and n are perpendicular, $z + w = 90$, and since lines m, n, and ℓ all intersect at the same point, angles directly across from each other are the same. This means that $w = x$ and $z + x = 90$ as well.

278. (C) The equation of the line through the given points can be found using the point slope formula: $y - y_1 = m(x - x_1)$ or $y - y_1 = \dfrac{y_2 - y_1}{x_2 - x_1}(x - x_1)$. Here, we find the equation of the line is $y = x + 5$. Any line parallel to this will have the same slope (1) and therefore not ever intersect this line. In other words, the lines cannot share any points. A review of the answer choices shows that all of the points except C are on the original line since they are of the form $(x, x + 5)$.

279. (A) When a point is reflected across the line, $y = x$, the x and y coordinates are interchanged.

280. 1. The total distance covered by the particle is the sum of the length of $\overline{PQ}$ and the length of $\overline{QR}$. Counting the units, $\overline{PQ}$ is 2 units long and $\overline{QR}$ is 3 units long, giving a total length of 5 units that the particle will cover in 1 second.

281. 8. The shortest distance would be the straight line distance, and the straight line distance from $(-8, 6)$ to the y-axis is 8.

282. **(A)** Using the point slope formula, the equation of line n is $y - (-1) = 2(x - (-2))$ or $y = 2x + 3$. Every point except the one in answer choice A is of the form $(x, 2x + 3)$.

283. **(C)** In 5 tick marks, we move from the origin to the point $(0, 30)$. This means the tick marks must count by 6, giving P the coordinates $(-18, 6)$.

284. **(B)** The slope of the described line is $\dfrac{6-2}{-2-8} = \dfrac{4}{-10} = -\dfrac{2}{5}$, and any line perpendicular to this line will have a slope of $\dfrac{5}{2}$. The slope of any line of the form $Ay + Bx = C$ is $-\dfrac{B}{A}$, and using this formula, we see the slope of the line in answer choice B is $\dfrac{5}{2}$.

285. 105. All of the angles lie along the line ℓ, therefore $x + 35 + 40 = 180$.

Chapter 5: Geometry

286. **(D)** The total measure of all angles within the triangle is 180 degrees. So, the measure of angle ACB is $180 - 90 - 55 = 35$. Angles ACB and BCD lie along the same line, so their sum must be 180, and angle BCD has a measure of $180 - 35 = 145$ degrees.

287. 3. If w is the width of the rectangle and l is the length, the perimeter is $2w + 2l = 8$. In this problem, we must find the smallest possible values of w and l such that this is true. Simplifying, this equation implies that $w + l = 4$, giving possible pairs of values of 1, 3 or 2, 2. With the first set of measurements, the area would be 3, and with the second the area would be 4.

288. **(C)** The figure is made of two rectangles. The rectangle on the left must have sides of length 3 and 6, giving it an area of 18. The rectangle on the right must have sides of length 4 and 5, giving it an area of 20. Therefore the total area is $18 + 20 = 38$ square units.

289. **(E)** The volume of each individual box is $2 \times 3 \times 10 = 60$ cubic inches. There are 40 of these boxes, so the container must have a volume of $40 \times 60 = 2,400$ cubic inches.

290. **(B)** If the circle is inscribed within the square, then the diameter must be 6 and the radius 3. Using the formula for the area of a circle, the area is $\pi(3)^2 = 9\pi$.

291. **(D)** All of the interior angles of ABC have a measure of 60 degrees, and since A and B are along a line, $3x = 180 - 60 = 120$ and $2y = 180 - 60 = 120$. Therefore, $x + y = 40 + 60 = 100$.

292. **(A)** Line segment $\overline{PQ}$ is the diameter of the circle, and since its length is 12, the radius of the circle is 6 and the area of the circle is 36π. Since the length of $\overline{AB}$ is 8, the area of the square is 64 and the area of the circle outside of the square is $36\pi - 64$. However, we are only interested in one of these 4 segments, so the area of the shaded region is $\frac{1}{4}$ of $36\pi - 64$ or $9\pi - 16$.

293. (E) Given the perimeter, we can write the equation $x + x + 2x + 2x = 18$ or $6x = 18$ and find that $x = 3$. Using the Pythagorean theorem, the length of diagonal $\overline{BD}$ is $\sqrt{3^2 + 6^2} = \sqrt{45} = 3\sqrt{5}$.

294. (C) Given $a = 70$, the remaining angle in that triangle is $180 - 2(70) = 40$ degrees. Similarly given $b = 80$, the remaining angle in that triangle is $180 - 2(80) = 20$ degrees. Finally, the sum of all the central angles must be 360, and this yields the formula $40 + 20 + c + \frac{3}{2}c = 360$ or $\frac{5}{2}c = 300$. This equation has a solution of $c = \frac{2}{5}(300) = 120$.

295. (B) Using the Pythagorean theorem, $x^2 + b^2 = 12^2$, where b is the distance from the bottom of the ladder to the building. Solving for b, $b^2 = 144 - x^2$ and $b = \sqrt{144 - x^2}$.

296. $\frac{3}{2}$. Using the formula for area of a triangle and the fact that ABC has twice the area of DEF, we can write the equation $\frac{1}{2}(4)b_1 = 2\left(\frac{1}{2}(3)b_2\right)$ or $2b_1 = 3b_2$. Manipulating this equation, $\frac{2b_1}{3b_2} = 1$ and $\frac{b_1}{b_2} = \frac{3}{2}$.

297. (A) All the sides of an equilateral triangle are the same length. If the length of $\overline{BC}$ is 4, then the length of $\overline{AC}$ is also 4, as is the length of $\overline{AB}$. Since M is the midpoint of $\overline{AC}$, the length of $\overline{AM}$ is 2. To find the perimeter of ABM, we need the length of $\overline{BM}$, which can be found using the Pythagorean theorem (ABM is a right triangle): $2^2 + (BM)^2 = 4^2$ or $BM = \sqrt{12} = 2\sqrt{3}$. Therefore, the perimeter is $2 + 4 + 2\sqrt{3} = 6 + 2\sqrt{3}$.

298. (A) The angle inside the unshaded segment is 36 degrees, which is $\frac{1}{10}$ the total angle (360) in the center of the circle. Since the area of the remaining $\frac{9}{10}$ of the circle is 90π, the area of the remaining segment must be 10π, giving a total area of 100π. If the area is 100π, then the radius must be $\sqrt{100} = 10$ and the circumference $2\pi r = 20\pi$. Finally, the length of the arc PQ will be $\frac{1}{10}$ this length or 2π.

299. 3. The given triangle is a right triangle, and further it is a 3-4-5 triangle since the legs have lengths $6 = 2(3)$ and $8 = 2(4)$. This triangle will have a hypotenuse of length $2(5) = 10$, so $4x - 2 = 10$ and $x = 3$.

300. (A) The area of rectangle 1 is $2k^2$, while the area of rectangle 2 is $6k^2 = 3(2k^2)$ so rectangle 2 is 3 times as large as rectangle 1.

301. (D) Given the radius of the smaller semicircle is 4, the area is $\frac{1}{2}(4^2)\pi = 8\pi$, leaving $40\pi - 8\pi = 32\pi$ as the area of the larger semicircle. For this semicircle, the radius can be found with the formula $\frac{1}{2}\pi r^2 = 32\pi$ or $\pi r^2 = 64\pi$. Therefore, the radius of this semicircle is 8 and the total distance from A to E is $4 + 4 + 8 + 8 = 24$.

302. (C) The shaded figure consists of the line segments $\overline{AB}$, $\overline{BC}$, $\overline{CR}$, $\overline{RQ}$, $\overline{QP}$, and $\overline{PA}$. Given the lengths of the sides of any equilateral triangle are the same, $AB = BC = 4$ and $PQ = QR = 2$. Since M is the midpoint of $\overline{AC}$ and $\overline{PR}$, $AP = RC = 1$, giving a perimeter of $4 + 4 + 1 + 2 + 2 + 1 = 14$.

303. (B) The portion of the circle that is shaded is $\frac{8\pi}{12\pi} = \frac{2}{3}$, leaving $\frac{1}{3}$ of the circle unshaded. The complete central angle of the circle is $360°$, so the unshaded portion will account for a third of this, or $120°$.

304. 54. Let the length of the rectangle be ℓ and the width be w. Given the information, we have two equations: $\ell = 6w$ and $2\ell + 2w = 42$. Plugging the first equation into the second, $2\ell + 2w = 2(6w) + 2w = 14w = 42$ and $w = 3$. The length is 6 times this value, so it is 18. We now can find the area: $\ell \times w = 18 \times 3 = 54$.

305. (D) Given that ABC is an equilateral triangle, sides $\overline{AB}$ and $\overline{AC}$ have a length of x. Further, given the right angle at point D, D must be the midpoint of $\overline{AC}$, giving $\overline{AD}$ and $\overline{DC}$ a length of $\frac{1}{2}x$. To find the perimeter of ABD, the only length we are missing is BD. This can be found using the Pythagorean theorem:

$$\left(\frac{1}{2}x\right)^2 + (BD)^2 = x^2$$

$$(BD)^2 = x^2 - \frac{1}{4}x^2 = \frac{3}{4}x^2$$

$$BD = \sqrt{\frac{3}{4}x^2} = \frac{\sqrt{3}}{2}x$$

With this length, the perimeter will be $AB + BD + AD = x + \frac{\sqrt{3}}{2}x + \frac{1}{2}x = \frac{2}{2}x + \frac{\sqrt{3}}{2}x + \frac{1}{2}x = \frac{3+\sqrt{3}}{2}x$.

306. (E) As shown in the following figure, we can draw a line on each end of the figure and create two equilateral triangles (since the resulting angles are $60°$). The base (and therefore all sides) of these triangles must be 2 units as shown by the dashed line. This means the polygon outlined by the solid line has 8 sides with length 2 and a perimeter of $8 \times 2 = 16$.

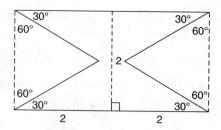

307. (E) The base angles of an isosceles triangle are always equal, so we can determine that angle *ABC* is also 70 degrees and angle *BCA* is 180 − 2(70) = 40 degrees. The angle opposite this will also have a measure of 40 degrees, leaving *x* = 180 − 40 − 20 = 120.

308. (A) If the length of the prism is ℓ, then the volume yields the formula $\ell wh = \dfrac{19}{2}$. Solving for ℓ: $\ell = \dfrac{19}{2wh}$.

309. (D) If the area of the circle is 32π, then the radius is $\sqrt{32} = 4\sqrt{2}$ and the diameter is $8\sqrt{2}$. Consider the diagonal $\overline{CE}$ (which is also a diameter). Since *BCDE* is a square, this diagonal is part of a 45-45-90 triangle *CBE* with sides 8, 8, $8\sqrt{2}$ and the area of the square is $8 \times 8 = 64$.

310. (E) The sum of the interior angles in a parallelogram is 360°, so *x* + *y* + *z* = 360 − 80 = 280.

311. (B) The sides of a cube all share the same length. If we let this length be *x*, then the volume is $x^3 = 27$ and *x* = 3. Therefore, the area of one face of the cube is $3 \times 3 = 9$ square meters, and five sides will have an area of $5 \times 9 = 45$ square meters. Since $\dfrac{45}{10} = 4.5$, we will need $4.5 \times 4 = 18$ gallons of paint.

312. (D) The central angle of any circle is 360 degrees, so angle *QOP* must have a measure of 60 degrees. Also, since $\overline{QR}$ and $\overline{QP}$ are tangent to the circle, angles *OQR* and *OPR* have measures of 90 degrees. Finally, *OQRP* is a quadrilateral and the sum of the interior angles must be 360 degrees, so *y* = 360 − 60 − 90 − 90 = 120 degrees.

313. (B) The three sides of any equilateral triangle have the same length, so the perimeter will be *z* + *z* + *z* = 3*z*.

314. (C) Let the length of $\overline{BC}$ be represented by *x*. Then the shaded region has an area of $2x - 2\left(\dfrac{1}{2}(2)(2)\right) = 2x - 4 = 24$, where $\dfrac{1}{2}(2)(2)$ is the area of *one* of the unshaded triangular regions. Solving this equation for *x*, we find that *x* = 14.

315. 10. If $AB = CB$, then ABC is an isosceles triangle and the angles opposite these sides must be equal. This means $x = 180 - 85 - 85 = 10$.

316. (A) As described, triangle ACD is equilateral with each side having a length of x, and since the half circle is centered at B, $AB = BC = \dfrac{x}{2}$. Line segment $\overline{AB}$ also acts as the radius, so the area of the half circle is $\pi\left(\dfrac{x}{2}\right)^2 = \dfrac{\pi x^2}{4}$.

317. (B) Since $AB = BF = AF$, angle $ABF = 60$ degrees. If angle FBD is a right angle (measure of 90 degrees), then since points A, B, and C lie on the same line, angle CBD has a measure of $180 - 60 - 90 = 30$ degrees.

318. 10. The perimeter would be the sum of 20 lengths and 2 widths of the smaller rectangles. Let these values be represented by ℓ and w, respectively, and we have the formulas $10\ell = 50$ and $20\ell + 2w = 104$. Using the first formula, $\ell = 5$, and by the second formula, $100 + 2w = 104$. Solving this, we find that $w = 2$. Therefore, the area of one of the smaller pieces of fabric is $5 \times 2 = 10$ square inches.

319. 16. Let the length be represented by ℓ and the width by w. The description states that when the length is $\ell + 8$, the area ℓw is 50% larger. Mathematically, $(\ell + 8)w = 1.5\ell w$. Solving for ℓ, $\ell + 8 = 1.5\ell$ and $8 = 0.5\ell$. Therefore, $\ell = 16$.

320. (E) The squares are congruent, meaning they are the same size. Therefore, all of the line segments in the figure have a length of 2. With a diameter of 2, the arcs BC and DE have a length of $\dfrac{1}{2}(2\pi) = \pi$, and the solid path has a length of $2 + 2\pi + 2 + 2\pi + 2 = 6 + 4\pi$.

321. 20. With the given information, we can write the equations $3a + 3b = 72$ and $a = \dfrac{1}{5}b$. Plugging the second equation into the first, $3\left(\dfrac{1}{5}b\right) + 3b = \dfrac{3}{5}b + \dfrac{15}{5}b = \dfrac{18}{5}b = 72$ or $b = 72\left(\dfrac{5}{18}\right) = 20$.

322. (A) The angle opposite y within the right triangle lies on the same line as the right angle and the 30-degree angle, so its measure is $180 - 30 - 90 = 60$ degrees. Similarly, the angle opposite x in the right triangle measures $180 - 90 - 35 = 55$ degrees. The two right triangles together create a quadrilateral with interior angles $90 + 55 = 145$, $90 + 60 = 150$, x, and y. Since the sum of the interior angles is 360 degrees, $x + y = 360 - 150 - 145 = 65$.

323. (A) The largest rectangle has an area of $3 \times 6 = 18$, while the central rectangle has an area of $3 \times 4 = 12$. Subtracting these leaves 6, the area of the left- and right-hand rectangles including the removed triangles. Each of the triangles has an area of $\dfrac{1}{2}(1)(1) = \dfrac{1}{2}$, so the area of the shaded region is $18 - 12 - 4\left(\dfrac{1}{2}\right) = 4$.

324. (A) Starting with the first tile, every other tile will be light colored. Along the length of the room, $\dfrac{40}{2} = 20$ tiles will be used, 10 of which are light colored. Along the width of the room, $\dfrac{120}{2} = 60$ tiles will be used, 30 of which are light colored. In other words, since the room has even dimensions, half the tiles will be light colored. The total area of the room is $40 \times 120 = 4,800$ square feet, so 2,400 square feet will be covered by light tiles.

325. (D) If D is the midpoint of $\overline{AB}$ and $\overline{AD}$ has a length of 2, then $\overline{AB}$ has a length of 4. The height of the triangle is a line from the apex to the midpoint of the base, so it is a leg of a right triangle with a hypotenuse of 4 (AB) and the other leg of 2. Using the Pythagorean theorem, $h^2 + 2^2 = 4^2$ and $h = \sqrt{12} = 2\sqrt{3}$. So, the area of triangle ABC is $\dfrac{1}{2}bh = \dfrac{1}{2}(4)(2\sqrt{3}) = 4\sqrt{3}$ where $b = AB$.

326. (C) The shortest distance from A to C is the diagonal of $ABCD$ or the hypotenuse of triangle ABD. Using the Pythagorean theorem, $x^2 + y^2 = d^2$.

327. (C) The area of circle 1 is $\pi\left(\dfrac{m}{2}\right)^2 = \dfrac{\pi m^2}{4}$, and the area of circle 2 is $(2m)^2\pi = 4m^2\pi$. We must multiply the area of circle 1 by 16 to get the area of circle 2.

328. (A) The figure is a triangle, so $180 = x + y + 85$ or $y = 95 - x$. Since angles y and z are along the same line, $y + z = 180$ or $z = 180 - y$. Combining equations, $z = 180 - y = 180 - (95 - x) = 180 - 95 + x = 85 + x$.

329. (A) If the length of one side of the square is x, then the radius of the circle is $\dfrac{x}{2}$. The area of the circle will be $\dfrac{\pi x^2}{4}$, and the area of the square will be x^2. Finally, the perimeter of the square will be $4x$ and the circumference of the circle will be πx. Notice that $\dfrac{\pi}{4}x^2 < x^2$ and $\pi x < 4x$ when $x > 1$.

330. (B) If $\overline{BD}$ bisects angle ABC, then the angle directly to the left of b is also 65 degrees. Since triangle ABD is a right triangle, $a = 180 - 90 - 65 = 25$.

331. (D) Since $ABCE$ is a square, triangle ABD is a right triangle and angle BDE must have a measure of $180 - 50 - 90 = 40$ degrees. This angle is also an interior angle of the triangle with base $\overline{ED}$ (also a right triangle). This means that the remaining angle in the triangle, lying on the same line as x, has a measure of $180 - 40 - 90 = 50$. Since these angles are on the same line, $x = 180 - 50 = 130$.

332. (C) Since DAB is an equilateral triangle, $AB = AD = y$. Further, since the angles opposite $\overline{BC}$ and $\overline{CD}$ have the same measure, $BC = CD = x$. The perimeter is then $2x + 2y = 2(x + y) = 18$. Solving for the term $x + y$, $x + y = \dfrac{18}{2} = 9$.

333. (D) The sides of a 45-45-90 triangle are always x, x, and $x\sqrt{2}$. In this case, $x = 3$ and the area is $\frac{1}{2}(3)(3) = \frac{9}{2}$.

334. (A) The two triangles given are isosceles, so it must be that angles BAC, BCA, DCE, and DEC have measures of 65 degrees. Angle BCD then has a measure of $180 - 65 - 65 = 50$ degrees.

335. (C) The volume of a cylinder is $\pi r^2 h$, where h is the height and r is the radius. Here, the total amount of water that can be held is the volume or $\pi(4^2)(10) = 160\pi$.

336. (D) The area of the complete ring is the difference between the areas of the circle with radius 9 and the circle with radius 5: $9^2\pi - 5^2\pi = 81\pi - 25\pi = 56\pi$. The shaded region makes up $\frac{105}{360} = \frac{7}{24}$ of the total area, so its area is $\frac{7}{24}(56\pi) = \frac{49\pi}{3}$.

337. 3. The total area of the gridded space is $2 \times 3 = 6$ square units. To find the area of the quadrilateral, we will subtract the area of the two triangles with hypotenuses $\overline{AB}$ and $\overline{CD}$. The triangle with hypotenuse $\overline{AB}$ has an area of $\frac{1}{2}(2)(2) = 2$ square units, while the triangle with hypotenuse $\overline{CD}$ has an area of $\frac{1}{2}(2)(1) = 1$ square unit. Therefore the area of $ABCD$ is $6 - 3 = 3$ square units.

338. (C) The right triangle that has $\overline{BC}$ as a hypotenuse is a 30-60-90 triangle, which always has legs of length x and $x\sqrt{3}$ and a hypotenuse of $2x$. In this case, $x = 4$ and $\overline{BC}$ has a length of $2(4) = 8$. Therefore the equilateral triangle ABC has a perimeter of $3 \times 8 = 24$.

339. 64. If the length of any side of the square is x, then by the Pythagorean theorem, $2x^2 = \left(8\sqrt{2}\right)^2$ and $x = 8$. Therefore, its area is $8 \times 8 = 64$.

340. (A) Since $ABCD$ is a parallelogram, angle ADC has a measure of 95 degrees. Since they lie along the same line, this means that angle CDE has a measure of $180 - 95 = 85$. Using the fact that the interior angles of a triangle must have a sum of 180 degrees, $x = 180 - 55 - 85 = 40$.

341. (E) The length of $\overline{AD}$ is 4, while the length of $\overline{DG}$ is 10. A line between A and G would be the hypotenuse of a right triangle with these line segments as legs. Using the Pythagorean theorem, $(AG)^2 = 4^2 + 10^2 = 116$ and $AG = \sqrt{116} = 2\sqrt{29}$.

342. (D) The perimeter will be the sum of 10 and the length of the arc AB since both $\overline{AO}$ and $\overline{OB}$ are radii of the circle. The interior angle of the segment is 40 degrees, so the length of the arc will be $\frac{40}{360}(2\pi(5)) = \frac{1}{9}(10\pi) = \frac{10\pi}{9}$. The perimeter is then $10 + \frac{10\pi}{9}$.

343. (E) If the area is x^2, then each side has a length of $\sqrt{x^2} = x$. There are four sides, so the perimeter will be $4x$.

344. (A) If the length of any side of the square $ABCD$ is s, then by the Pythagorean theorem, $2s^2 = x^2$ and $s = \sqrt{\dfrac{x^2}{2}} = \dfrac{x}{\sqrt{2}} = \dfrac{x\sqrt{2}}{2}$. The volume is then $\left(\dfrac{x\sqrt{2}}{2}\right)^3 = \dfrac{x^3(2\sqrt{2})}{8} = \dfrac{x^3\sqrt{2}}{4}$.

345. 8. If r is the radius of the original circle, then $\pi\left(\dfrac{r}{2}\right)^2 = 16\pi$ and $\dfrac{r}{2} = 4$, so $r = 8$.

346. (B) Let A be the circumference of circle A and B be the circumference of circle B. The given information can be used to write the equation $A = 3B$, which is equivalent to $2\pi r = 3(2\pi b)$ where b is the radius of circle B. Solving for b: $b = \dfrac{2\pi r}{6\pi} = \dfrac{r}{3}$.

347. 16. If x is a side of the square, then the triangle has area $\dfrac{1}{2}(x)(x) = 8$ or $x^2 = 16$. Therefore each side has a length of 4 and the perimeter is $4 \times 4 = 16$.

348. (A) Since E is the midpoint of $\overline{AD}$, $AE = ED = 6$. Using the area of triangle ABE, $\dfrac{1}{2}(6)(BE) = 21$ or $BE = 7$. Using the area of ECD, $\dfrac{1}{2}(6)(CE) = 30$ or CE = 10. Therefore, $x = 10 - 7 = 3$.

349. (D) The square $ABCD$ has an area of $10 \times 10 = 100$, and the quarter circle has an area of $\left(\dfrac{1}{4}\right)\pi(10^2) = 25\pi$, leaving the shaded region with an area of $100 - 25\pi$.

350. (B) If C is the midpoint of $\overline{BD}$ and $BC = 2$, then $BD = 4$ and every other side also has a length of 4. The triangle ACE then has a base of 4 and a height equal to the length of $\overline{AB}$, which is also 4, yielding an area of $\dfrac{1}{2}(4)(4) = 8$.

351. (C) Point A will be connected to each of the 5 other points.

352. 343. There are 6 faces to a cube, so each square that makes up this cube has an area of $\dfrac{294}{6} = 49$. If each face is a square with sides of length x, then the area is $x^2 = 49$ and $x = \sqrt{49} = 7$. The volume is then $x^3 = 7^3 = 343$.

353. (B) The largest such triangle would use a main diagonal as its hypotenuse and have a base and height equal to the width and length of the rectangle. Therefore, its area would be $\dfrac{1}{2}(3)(8) = 12$.

354. (C) If r is the radius of the circle, then $\dfrac{30}{360}\pi r^2 = \dfrac{\pi r^2}{12} = 3\pi$ is the area of the shaded region of the circle. Solving this equation for r, we get $r = 6$ and a diameter of $2r = 12$.

355. (E) If x is the length of a single side of the square and r is the radius of the circle, then $P = \dfrac{C}{\pi}$ can be written as $4x = \dfrac{2\pi r}{\pi} = 2r$. This gives us the equation $x = \dfrac{r}{2}$. The area of the circle would then be $A_C = \pi r^2$ and the area of the square $A_S = x^2 = \dfrac{r^2}{4} = \dfrac{\pi r^2}{4\pi} = \dfrac{A_C}{4\pi}$.

356. (A) Let w and l be the common width and length. If x is the length of prism A and y is the length of prism B, then the volume of A is xlw while the volume of B is ylw. But $x = \dfrac{1}{3}y$, so the volume of A is $xlw = \dfrac{1}{3}ylw$. Calculating and simplifying the ratio:

$$\dfrac{1}{3}ylw : ylw \Leftrightarrow \dfrac{1}{3} : 1 \Leftrightarrow 1 : 3.$$

357. (B) Since GCF is an equilateral triangle, angles BFA and EGD both have a measure of 60 degrees. Since ABF and GDE are right triangles, both x and y are equal to $180 - 90 - 60 = 30$, so $x + y = 30 + 30 = 60$.

358. (B) Using the circumference formula, the length of arc AC is $\dfrac{1}{2}(2\pi x) = \pi x$ and the length of arc CE is $\dfrac{1}{2}(2\pi(2x)) = 2\pi x$. The total length of the path is then $\pi x + 2\pi x = 3\pi x$.

Chapter 6: Proportions

359. (B) Let r be the number of red marbles and g be the number of green marbles. There are only two colors, so it must be that $r + g = 800$. Given the ratio, it must also be true that $\dfrac{r}{g} = \dfrac{2}{3}$ or $g = \dfrac{3}{2}r$. Plugging this into the first equation, $r + g = r + \dfrac{3}{2}r = \dfrac{5}{2}r = 800$ and $r = 800\left(\dfrac{2}{5}\right) = 320$.

360. (A) 75% or $0.75x$ regularly attend meetings, and of these, 20% or $0.2(0.75)x = 0.15x$ are also considered senior members.

361. (A) $\dfrac{x}{100}(125) = \dfrac{x}{4}(5) = \dfrac{5x}{4}$.

362. (A) Since 15 minutes is $\dfrac{15}{60} = \dfrac{1}{4}$ hour, the vehicle will travel one-fourth of the distance.

363. (D) The length of B is 5 times the length of A; therefore the width of B will be 5 times the width of A.

364. (D) For some k, $y = kx$. Given the initial values, $c^2 = k\left(\dfrac{c}{2}\right)$ and $2c^2 = kc$. Since c is nonzero, $k = 2c$, and when $x = 5$, $y = 2c(5) = 10c$.

365. (C) $\dfrac{45}{100}(6x + 10y) = \dfrac{9}{20}(6x + 10y) = \dfrac{9}{10}(3x + 5y) = \dfrac{27x + 45y}{10}$.

366. (B) If x is the original price of a single piece of the furniture, $5(1.25)x = 675$ and $x = 108$.

367. (B) The team had $0.4(80) = 32$ home games. If it won W of these and lost L of these, $W + L = 32$ and $3L = W$. When we plug the second equation into the first, we find that $4L = 32$ and $L = 8$.

368. (B) $\dfrac{a+b}{b} = \dfrac{a}{b} + 1 = \dfrac{3}{11} + 1 = \dfrac{14}{11}$.

369. (C) For some k, $m = \dfrac{n}{k}$, and using the given values, $5 = \dfrac{1}{k}$ and $k = \dfrac{1}{5}$. Therefore when $n = x$, $m = \dfrac{x}{\frac{1}{5}} = 5x$.

370. (C) If the number has a nonzero remainder when divided by k, it is not divisible by k; 60% of the numbers in this set have that property and $\dfrac{60}{100} = \dfrac{3}{5}$.

371. (D) If x is increased by 40%, then the resulting value is $1.4x$ and this is equal to 92. Therefore $x = \dfrac{92}{1.4} = \dfrac{460}{7}$. Decreasing this by 10%: $0.9x = \dfrac{90}{100}\left(\dfrac{460}{7}\right) = \dfrac{414}{7}$.

372. (B) Let B represent the number of blue cards and G represent the number of green cards. Then, $B + G = 200$ and $B = G + 54$. This means $B + G = G + G + 54 = 200$, or $2G = 146$ and $G = 73$. Finally, $\dfrac{73}{200} = 0.365$.

373. (C) If J is the number of juniors and S is the number of seniors, then $J + S = $ total, and given the ratio, $3J = S$. Therefore $4J = $ total, indicating the total must be divisible by 4, and 58 is not.

374. 15.21. The cost of a single share originally was $\dfrac{140.6}{10} = 14.06$. When it increased by 3%, it was worth $1.03(14.06) = 14.48$, and then after it increased by 5%, it was worth $1.05(1.03(14.06)) = 1.05(14.48) = 15.21$.

375. $\dfrac{15}{8}$. If S is the amount of sugar to use, $\dfrac{\frac{5}{4}}{S} = \dfrac{2}{3}$ and $2S = \dfrac{15}{4}$. Therefore $S = \left(\dfrac{1}{2}\right)\dfrac{15}{4} = \dfrac{15}{8}$.

376. (E) $\frac{1}{4}\%$ of x is equivalent to $0.0025x$, so $0.0025x = 19$ and $x = 7,600$.

377. (B) For some k, $a = kb$, and given the initial values, $18 = 3k$ or $k = 6$. Therefore when $b = \frac{1}{3}$, $a = 6\left(\frac{1}{3}\right) = 2$.

378. (C) For some k, $y = kx$, and given the initial values, $4 = k\sqrt{2}$ or $k = 2\sqrt{2}$. Therefore the first equation can be rewritten as $y = 2x\sqrt{2}$.

379. 0.75. If x is the length of the scale model, then $\frac{x}{60} = \frac{1}{80}$ and $x = \frac{60}{80} = 0.75$.

380. (C) $\frac{85}{100}\left(\frac{2}{100}\right)x = \frac{170x}{10,000} = \frac{17x}{1,000}$.

381. (E) $\left(\frac{48 \text{ lines}}{40 \text{ min}}\right)(210 \text{ min}) = \left(\frac{1.2 \text{ lines}}{\text{min}}\right)(210 \text{ min}) = 252 \text{ lines}$.

382. (C) If b is the base of triangle A and h is its height, then its area is $\frac{1}{2}bh$. The area of triangle B is then $\frac{1}{2}(3h)(3b) = \frac{9}{2}bh$ and the ratio is $1 : 9$.

383. (B) $\frac{1}{8}\% = 0.00125$ and $0.00125(2,115) = 2.64$. Since x is an integer and larger than this value, x must be 3.

384. (B) In 100 minutes, Bobby can run $5 \times 3 = 15$ miles and Aiden can run $4 \times 3 = 12$ miles. The difference is 3 miles.

385. (D) Cross multiply: $\frac{x}{y} = \frac{2}{7}$.

386. (A) $\frac{a}{b}\% = \frac{\frac{a}{b}}{100} = \frac{a}{100b}$ and $\frac{a}{100b}(100) = \frac{a}{b}$.

387. 13.4%. $100\left(\frac{34.86 - 30.19}{34.86}\right) = 13.4$.

388. (E) Tutor A has an hourly rate of $\frac{90}{3} = \$30$. Therefore the ratio is $30 : 40$ or $3 : 4$.

389. 18. For some k, $m = kn$, but since $m = 6a$ when $n = a$, $k = 6$. When $n = 3$, $m = 6(3) = 18$.

390. 600. If $0.8x = 480$, then $x = \frac{480}{0.8} = 600$.

391. 10.8. Suppose x is the one-way distance from her house to the grocery store. Then it took her $\left(\dfrac{1 \text{ hour}}{12 \text{ miles}}\right) x \text{ miles} = \dfrac{x}{12}$ hours to make the trip there and similarly $\dfrac{x}{18}$ hours to make the trip back. The total trip was 45 minutes or 0.75 hours, so $\dfrac{x}{12} + \dfrac{x}{18} = 0.75$, and multiplying both sides by 36 we have $5x = 27$. We find the solution to this equation is $\dfrac{27}{5} = 5.4$ miles. If the one-way distance is 5.4 miles, then the round-trip distance is $2(5.4) = 10.8$ miles.

392. **(A)** If x represents the number of dinner plates and y represents the number of dessert plates, then we have the equations $x + y = n$ and $\dfrac{x}{y} = \dfrac{5}{3}$. Solving the second equation for y, we have $y = \dfrac{3}{5}x$. Using this in the first equation, $x + y = x + \dfrac{3}{5}x = \dfrac{8}{5}x = n$ and $x = \dfrac{5n}{8}$.

393. **(C)** $100\left(\dfrac{x}{5x}\right) = 100\left(\dfrac{1}{5}\right) = 20$.

394. 52. For some constant k, $b = k(a^2 + 1)$, and using the given values, $10 = k(4 + 1)$ or $k = 2$. Therefore, when $a = 5$, $b = 2(5^2 + 1) = 2(26) = 52$.

395. **(D)** Both described triangles must be 30-60-90 triangles, whose legs always have lengths x and $x\sqrt{3}$. The hypotenuse of these types of triangles is always $2x$, and in triangle A, $x = 4$, while in triangle B, $x = 1$. Therefore the legs of triangle A are 4 and $4\sqrt{3}$, while the sides of triangle B are 1 and $\sqrt{3}$. The areas are then $\dfrac{1}{2}(8)\left(4\sqrt{3}\right) = 16\sqrt{3}$ for triangle A and $\dfrac{1}{2}(1)\sqrt{3} = \dfrac{\sqrt{3}}{2}$ for triangle B, giving a ratio of $16 : \dfrac{1}{2}$ or $32 : 1$.

396. **(D)** The price will be 90% of its original or $\dfrac{90}{100}m = \dfrac{9}{10}m$ dollars.

397. **(B)** $\dfrac{\frac{1}{x}}{100}\left(\dfrac{25}{y}\right) = \dfrac{1}{100x}\left(\dfrac{25}{y}\right) = \dfrac{1}{4xy}$.

398. 57.49. If x is the original price, then $0.8x = 45.99$ and $x = \dfrac{45.99}{0.8} = 57.49$ dollars.

399. **(A)** After decreasing by 12%, x retains 88% of its value, so $0.88x = a$. An increase of 10% is equivalent to $x + 0.1x = 1.1x$, so $b = 1.1x$ and $a - b = 0.88x - 1.1x = -0.22x$.

400. **(D)** 0.06% is equivalent to $\dfrac{0.06}{100} = 0.0006$, and if $0.0006x = 6$, then $x = \dfrac{6}{0.0006} = 10{,}000$.

401. (D) $\left(\dfrac{2 \text{ machines}}{3 \text{ days}}\right) \times (20 \text{ days}) = 13.33$ machines or 13 complete machines.

402. $\dfrac{250}{41}$. As an equation, the given information can be written as $\dfrac{c}{100}(18) = c - 5$, which is equivalent to $\dfrac{9c}{50} = c - 5$. Cross multiplying, we find $50c - 250 = 9c$ or $41c = 250$, so $c = \dfrac{250}{41}$.

403. (A) The area of a single face would be x^2, while the volume of the cube would be x^3, so the ratio is $x^2 : x^3$, which is equivalent to $1 : x$.

404. (A) Given the ratio, the equation $\dfrac{m}{n} = \dfrac{2}{9}$ must be true and $\dfrac{18m}{n} = 18\left(\dfrac{m}{n}\right) = 18\left(\dfrac{2}{9}\right) = \dfrac{4}{1}$.

405. (E) Let R be the number of red marbles and B the number of blue. Since there are 15% more red marbles, $R = B + 0.15B = 1.15B$ and the total is $R + B = 1.15B + B = 2.15B$. Since we cannot have a fractional number of marbles, the total number must be divisible by 2.15 and $200(2.15) = 430$.

406. 48. For some constant k, $t = \dfrac{k}{r}$, and given the initial values $6 = \dfrac{k}{2}$ and $k = 12$. Therefore when $r = \dfrac{1}{4}$, $t = \dfrac{12}{\frac{1}{4}} = 48$.

407. 280. If $0.25x - 0.2x = 14$, then $0.05x = 14$ and $x = \dfrac{14}{.05} = 280$.

408. (C) Given the ratio, if Frank's hourly pay is F and Rich's is R, then $\dfrac{F}{R} = \dfrac{5}{6}$ or $5R = 6F$. Further, after two hours of work, they will be paid $2(F + R) = 66$, which is equivalent to $F + R = 33$. Using the first equation, $F = \dfrac{5}{6}R$, and given the second equation, $F + R = \dfrac{5}{6}R + R = \dfrac{11}{6}R = 33$. Finally, $R = 33\left(\dfrac{6}{11}\right) = 18$.

409. (C) For some constant k, $y = \dfrac{k}{x}$, and given the initial values, $\dfrac{1}{3}n = \dfrac{k}{12n}$ or $k = 4n^2$. Therefore when $x = 2n$, $y = \dfrac{4n^2}{2n} = 2n$.

410. (D) If $\dfrac{x}{100}(y) = \dfrac{xy}{100} = a$, then $\dfrac{y}{100}(x) = \dfrac{xy}{100} = a$ as well.

411. (D) $100\left(\dfrac{155 - 135}{135}\right) = 14.8$.

412. (B) The sides of the original garden are $\sqrt{62,500} = 250$ feet, which would be $\frac{250}{100} = 2.5$ feet in the model. Therefore in the model, the area will be $2.5 \times 2.5 = 6.25$ square feet.

413. (A) $\frac{x \text{ nails}}{6 \text{ hours}} \times 20 \text{ hours} = \frac{20x}{6} \text{ nails} = \frac{10x}{3} \text{ nails.}$

414. (B) Since they are directly proportional, if E is the number of employees required and C is the number of customers, $E = kC$ for some constant k. Using the initial data, $20 = k(850)$ and $k = \frac{2}{85}$. Therefore, given 340 customers, $E = \frac{2}{85}(340) = 8$.

415. (B) $5 : 15$, which is equivalent to $1 : 3$.

416. (C) After the three changed their minds, there are $x - 3$ remaining who think green is their favorite color. The total number of first graders did not change, so the percentage is $100\left(\frac{x-3}{y}\right) = \frac{100(x-3)}{y}\%$.

417. (C) $\frac{x+y}{100}\left(\frac{50}{x^2 + 2xy + y^2}\right) = \frac{x+y}{2}\left(\frac{1}{(x+y)(x+y)}\right) = \frac{1}{2}\left(\frac{1}{x+y}\right) = \frac{1}{2(x+y)}$.

418. (B) $(100 - 64)\% = 36\%$ received a lower grade, and $\frac{36}{100} = \frac{9}{25}$.

419. $\frac{221}{6}$. The equation $\frac{\frac{13}{2}}{b} = \frac{3}{17}$ is equivalent to $3b = \frac{221}{2}$ and $b = \frac{221}{6}$.

420. (E) If the initial value was V, then after the first year the value was $0.92V$. After the second year, the value was $0.98(0.92)V = 90.16V$. Therefore, it retained 90.2% of its initial value.

421. (B) If there was a 5% increase, there would be $1.05(250) = 262.5$ members, and if there was a 10% increase, there would be $1.1(250) = 275$ members. Since the percentage increase was between 5% and 10%, the number of members after the increase must be between 262.5 and 275 (not inclusive).

422. (E) Since $5(0.03) = .15$, 3% of the number will be $\frac{35}{5} = 7$.

423. (C) On sale, item A costs 90% of its original price or $\$\frac{9m}{10}$, while item B costs 80% of its original price or $\$\frac{8n}{10}$. Together, they cost $\frac{9m+8n}{10}$ dollars.

424. (A) $x = \frac{5}{100}\left(\frac{1}{4}\right) = \frac{5}{400} = \frac{1}{80}$.

425. 85. $(100 - 10 - 40)\% = 50\%$ of the jackets will be large and $0.5(170) = 85$.

426. **(E)** By cross multiplying we see $8x = y$ and $8 = \dfrac{y}{x}$. Multiplying by 100 gives us the percentage.

427. $\dfrac{5}{2}$. Using the ratio, $\dfrac{x}{y} = \dfrac{1}{3}$, and if $y = x + 1$, $\dfrac{x}{x+1} = \dfrac{1}{3}$, which is equivalent to $3x = x+1$. Solving this, we see that $x = \dfrac{1}{2}$ and $z = 5\left(\dfrac{1}{2}\right) = \dfrac{5}{2}$.

428. **(C)** After 50 minutes, the particle will have moved $\left(\dfrac{4 \text{ units}}{20 \text{ min}}\right)(50 \text{ min}) = 10$ units. Starting at the origin and moving along the x-axis, this would lead us 10 units away from $(0, 0)$ to $(10, 0)$.

Chapter 7: Functions

429. **(D)** If $x(x + 4)(x - 4) = 0$, then the function is equal to zero at $x = 0$, $x = -4$, and $x = 4$.

430. **(A)** Because of its form, the graph is a parabola, and since the sign on the squared term is negative, the parabola opens downward. Further, it is a translation of $f(x) = x^2$, so its highest point will be its y-intercept, -5.

431. **(C)** Using the zero-product rule, $a^3 = 0$ or $a^2 - 1 = 0$. From the first equation, we have $a = 0$, and from the second, $a = \pm\sqrt{1} = \pm 1$.

432. **(C)** $f(c + 1) = (c + 1)^2 - (c + 1) = c^2 + 2c + 1 - c - 1 = c^2 + c$.

433. 5. The given equation is equivalent to $3x^2 - 16x + 5 = 0$, which by factoring is equivalent to $(3x - 1)(x - 5) = 0$. Using the zero product rule, the two solutions are $x = \dfrac{1}{3}$, $x = 5$.

434. **(A)** $g(-1) = \dfrac{-1-6}{(-1)^2} = \dfrac{-7}{1} = -7$.

435. **(E)** $f\left(\dfrac{1}{8}k + 6\right) = \left(\dfrac{1}{8}k + 6\right) + 5 = \dfrac{1}{8}k + 11$.

436. **(D)** The graph of $f(x - 2)$ is the graph of $f(x)$ translated by 2 units to the right (horizontal translation).

437. **(E)** On the ends, the function is defined where there are solid circles. Therefore $f(1) = 2$ and $f(3) = 4$.

438. **(D)** Since the graph is opening up, the sign of a must be positive. Also, since the graph is not centered along the y-axis, it isn't a translation of x^2, so b is nonzero.

439. **(E)** The function is greater than zero anywhere the graph is above the x-axis.

440. (B) To have x-intercepts at those points, it must be that $f(x) = (x-4)(x+3) = x^2 - x - 12$. Here, the coefficient on x is -1, which means that $b = -1$.

441. (E) When $n = 2$, $f(n) = f(2) = 2 - 8 = -6$, so if $n > 2$, $f(n) > -6$.

442. (B) If $g(k+1) = \dfrac{(k+1)+1}{k+1} = \dfrac{k+2}{k+1} = 3$, then by cross multiplying we see that $3(k+1)$ $= k + 2$, or $3k + 3 = k + 2$. Solving this equation, we find $2k = -1$ or $k = -\dfrac{1}{2}$.

443. (D) Since 1 is odd and 2 is even, $k(1) + k(2) = 6 + 4 = 10$.

444. (A) Each point was moved three units to the right. This is a horizontal translation of $f(x)$ and has the form $f(x-3)$.

445. (A) The correct equation has a value of -4 when $x = 0$ and a negative value on the squared term as the graph must be facing downward to not cross the x-axis when the vertex is at $(0, -4)$.

446. 1. The function has only two values: 2 and -3. If $f(x) > 1$, it must be that $f(x) = 2$. The smallest positive integer where this is true is $x = 1$.

447. (E) The graph of $g(x)$ is just a vertical translation of the graph of $f(x)$, so the slope will remain the same.

448. (D) Points A and C are x-intercepts of $h(x)$, so to find them we must solve $x^2 - 8 = 0$. This has solutions $x = \pm\sqrt{8} = \pm 2\sqrt{2}$. For the triangle, the distance from A to C is $2\sqrt{2} + 2\sqrt{2} = 4\sqrt{2}$ and the height is the line from the origin to B, which has a length of 5. The area is thus $\dfrac{1}{2}(4\sqrt{2})(5) = 10\sqrt{2}$.

449. (C) $f(-1) = (-1)^4 - 4(-1) = 1 + 4 = 5$.

450. (B) The graph of $h(x)$ is a vertical translation of the graph of $g(x)$. In this case, the graph would be moved down by k units. This means every point's y-coordinate will be lowered by k units as we see in choice B.

451. (C) If the two functions intersect at that point, then $f(x) = g(x)$ at that point. In other words, $\left(\dfrac{\sqrt{2}}{2}\right)^2 + 1 = k\left(\dfrac{\sqrt{2}}{2}\right)^2$ and $\dfrac{1}{2} + 1 = \dfrac{1}{2}k$. Thus $\dfrac{3}{2} = \dfrac{1}{2}k$ and $k = 3$.

452. (C) $g(4) = \dfrac{1}{2}f(4) + 4 = \dfrac{1}{2}(3(4)^2 - 4) + 4 = \dfrac{1}{2}(44) + 4 = 22 + 4 = 26$.

453. (E) The question is asking us to find the coordinates of the vertex. The first coordinate will be h, the hour where the most code was written, and the second coordinate will be c, the number of lines of code written in that hour. The first coordinate of the vertex is $\frac{-b}{2a} = -\frac{-12}{2(-1)} = 6$, which we use to find the second coordinate: $c(6) = -(6)^2 + 12(6) = 36$.

454. (B) $V(8) = 5,000(0.92)^8 = 2,566.09$.

455. 27. If $(3, 9)$ is on the line, then $f(3) = 9$. Therefore, $(3)^3 + (3)^2 - n = 9$ or $36 - n = 9$. Finally, $n = 27$.

456. (B) Setting the function equal to zero, the graph will cross the x-axis at the points with x-coordinates 4, −1, −6, and 9.

457. (C) If $h(x+3) = \dfrac{x+3-1}{4} = \dfrac{x+2}{4} = 5$, then $x + 2 = 20$ and $x = 18$.

458. (E) The graph of $f(x) - 6$ will be a vertical translation of $f(x)$. The point $(4, 0)$ will be translated to the point $(4, -6)$, but there is no way to determine which point will be translated onto the x-axis without more information about the function.

459. (C) If $g(x) = 0$, then $x = 0$ or $x = 1$ by the zero product rule.

460. 2. $\dfrac{8}{3}$ is between 2 and 3, and reading from that area up to the function shows the function is at the value 2 between $x = 2$ and $x = 3$.

461. (D) The line $x + 4$ has a positive slope, and as part of $f(x)$ will reach its highest point at values just before $x = 1$. When $x = 1$, $x + 4 = 5$. Although the function will not reach this value, it will have a value between 4 (the y-intercept) and 5 when x is between 0 and 1. After $x = 1$, $f(x) = 3$, and before $x = 0$, $f(x) < 4$.

462. 1.6. $f(1.2) = \dfrac{1.2}{2} + 1 = 1.6$.

463. (D) The given values are x-intercepts, which implies −2 and 6 are zeros of the function. Therefore the function would be $f(x) = (x+2)(x-6) = x^2 - 4x - 12$.

464. (A) $g(f(x)) = \dfrac{1}{2} f(x) + \dfrac{1}{2} = \dfrac{1}{2}\left(\dfrac{4}{5} x^2\right) + \dfrac{1}{2} = \dfrac{2}{5} x^2 + \dfrac{1}{2}$.

465. (E) The graph of the function never goes above the line $y = 3$. However, since it does reach that point, the inequality $f(x) < 3$ is not true for ALL values of x. Instead, we must have a value larger than 3 on the right-hand side of this inequality for it to be true.

466. (D) Any vertical translation of $-x^2 + 1$ is a vertical translation of $-x^2$, which has its maximum value along the y-axis. Since the graph is only moved vertically, this will remain true.

467. (C) By the zero product rule, $x^3 = 0$ and $x^2 - 4x + 4 = (x-2)^2 = 0$. Solving these equations, we see the roots of the larger equation are 0 and 2.

468. (E) The equation $n^2 - 8n = 9$ is equivalent to the equation $n^2 - 8n - 9 = 0$. Further, by factoring, we see this equation is equivalent to $(x - 9)(x + 1) = 0$. By the zero product rule, $x - 9 = 0$ and $x + 1 = 0$, so the solutions are 9 and -1. The sum of these numbers is 8.

469. (C) The function $f(x)$ is greater than zero whenever its graph is above the x-axis. This occurs between $x = -3$ and $x = 3$.

470. (B) The graph will be a parabola, so it will have either a single minimum or a single maximum. Since a is positive, the graph will open up and will have a single minimum value. Because the minimum may occur above the x-axis, we cannot say if it crosses the x-axis or not.

471. (A) The graphs will intersect when $x^2 + 3x - 8 = -4$ or $x^2 + 3x - 4 = 0$. Factoring, this equation is equivalent to $(x + 4)(x - 1) = 0$, which by the zero product rule indicates $x = -4$ or $x = 1$. Thus $n = 1$ would be the largest x-coordinate possible.

472. (B) Using the equation $5f(x) = f(x)$, $5(3x - 1) = 3x - 1$ and $15x - 5 = 3x - 1$. Collecting like terms, this is equivalent to $12x = 4$ and $x = \dfrac{4}{12} = \dfrac{1}{3}$.

473. (E) $g(-2) = 2(-2) - (-2)^3 = -4 - (-8) = -4 + 8 = 4$.

474. (A) The graph must be opening up, therefore $a > 0$.

475. (B) If $f(x) > 2$ for all values of x, the entire graph must be above the line $y = 2$. All graphs other than the graph in answer choice B cross or touch this line at some point.

476. (E) $f(2a - 1) = \dfrac{(2a - 1)^2 - (2a - 1)}{2} = \dfrac{4a^2 - 4a + 1 - 2a + 1}{2} = \dfrac{4a^2 - 6a + 2}{2} = 2a^2 - 3a + 1$.

477. (A) If $c = 0$, then $f(c) = -9$. Therefore, if $c > 0$, $f(c) > -9$.

478. 8. The graph would be translated up by 6 units. Therefore, the y-coordinate of every point would be 6 units larger.

479. 24. $f(t) = -2(2)^2 + 32 = -2(4) + 32 = -8 + 32 = 24$.

480. (C) If $g(0) = 10$, then $c = 10$. Using this, $g(-1) = (-1)^3 - k(-1) + 10 = -1 + k + 10$, giving us the equation $k + 9 = 4$. Therefore, $k = -5$ and $k + c = -5 + 10 = 5$.

481. 6. The zeros of the function occur at -2 and -1. Therefore, the function is $(x + 2)(x + 1) = x^2 + 3x + 2$ and $bc = 3(2) = 6$.

482. (C) If $f(x) = -f(x)$, then $-x^2 + 10x - 21 = x^2 - 10x + 21$. Collecting like terms, this is equivalent to $2x^2 - 20x + 42 = 2(x^2 - 10x + 21) = 2(x - 7)(x - 3) = 0$. Therefore, the functions intersect when $x = 7$ and $x = 3$.

483. 7. $f\left(\sqrt{k}\right) = 35 = 5\left(\sqrt{k}\right)\sqrt{k} = 5k$ and $k = \dfrac{35}{5} = 7.$

484. (C) $y = h(3) = 4(3)^2 - 3^3 = 4(9) - 27 = 9.$

485. (D) If $f(2m+1) = 3m$, then since $(2m+1)^2 - 3 = 4m^2 + 4m + 1 - 3 = 4m^2 + 4m - 2$, $4m^2 + 4m - 2 = 3m$. Subtracting $3m$ from both sides and adding 2 to both sides, we get $4m^2 + m = 2.$

486. (E) $g(4k) = g\left(\dfrac{8k}{2}\right) = 3(8k) - 2 = 24k - 2.$

487. 15. The value of the function at $x = 4$ is located where the solid circle is. Therefore $f(4) + f(7) = 6 + 9 = 15.$

488. (E) The only change in the points is that the x-coordinate was reduced by 5 units. This means that $m = 5$. Since the y-coordinate did not change, $n = 0$ and $m + n = 5.$

489. (E) Using the definitions of f and g, the equation given is equivalent to $\dfrac{a-1}{6} = \dfrac{1}{a-2}.$ Cross multiplying, $(a - 1)(a - 2) = 6$ and $a^2 - 3a + 2 = 6$. Finally by subtracting 6 from both sides and factoring we have $(a - 4)(a + 1) = 0$, which has roots 4 and -1.

490. (B) As described, $f(x) = (x - 3)^2 + 4$. Simplifying this expression by using the FOIL method, $f(x) = x^2 - 6x + 9 + 4 = x^2 - 6x + 13.$

491. (C) We are given the y value, which is the value of the function when x is plugged in. Therefore $\dfrac{1}{2}(x - 1)^2 = \dfrac{3}{2}$, and multiplying by 2, this is equivalent to $(x - 1)^2 = 3$. Using the square root rule, $x - 1 = \pm\sqrt{3}$ and $x = 1 \pm \sqrt{3}$. Since x is positive, $x = 1 + \sqrt{3}.$

492. (A) Plugging in the given point, $8 = c(-2)^3$ or $8 = -8c$. Therefore, $c = \dfrac{8}{-8} = -1.$

493. (B) When $f(x) = 2$, it doesn't imply anything about when $x = 2$. Therefore, choice III may or may not be true. Additionally, the fact that $f(x)$ never crosses $y = 2$ simply means there is no x such that $f(x) = 2$, by definition. It may be that the graph crosses the x-axis once or even more.

494. 24. Given the equation, $g(a) = \dfrac{f(a)}{8}$. Further $g(a) = 3$, so $3 = \dfrac{f(a)}{8}$ and $f(a) = 3 \times 8 = 24.$

495. (B) When $x > 1$, $x - 1$ is positive and its absolute value will have the same value. Therefore when $x > 1$, $g(x) = \dfrac{x-1}{x-1} = 1.$

496. (E) We must have the definition of the function to determine the value of $f(13)$. While $f(12) = 12 - 1$, the same pattern may not hold for all possible inputs.

497. (A) Given $f(x)$, the graph of $f(x+1)$ will be the graph of $f(x)$ translated to the left one unit. Translating this graph up four units will result in the graph of $f(x+1)+4$.

498. 18. $\dfrac{(f(2))^2}{2} = \dfrac{(2+2^2)^2}{2} = \dfrac{(2+4)^2}{2} = \dfrac{6^2}{2} = \dfrac{36}{2} = 18.$

499. (D) The graphs intersect at any point (x, y) where $-x^2 + 9 = x^2 - 9$. Solving this equation, $2x^2 - 18 = 0$ and $2(x+3)(x-3) = 0$. Therefore the possible x coordinates are -3 and 3. However, we only keep 3 since x and y are nonnegative. Finally, since $f(3) = 0$, $x + y = 3 + 0 = 3$.

500. 56. The value of b is the value of the y coordinate when $x = 10$. Using the equation for $g(x)$, $b = \dfrac{1}{2}(10)^2 + 6 = 56$.